Shortly afterwards he was received into his true spiritual home, the Church of England, and ordained by Archbishop Temple. He spent happy years writing, preaching and in parish duties before he died in 1958, leaving this autobiography among his papers.

He tells the story of his pilgrimage with great vividness and honesty, and a rare willingness to face the implications of his actions and beliefs.

IN SEARCH OF MYSELF

IN SEARCH OF MYSELF

The Autobiography of
D. R. DAVIES

GEOFFREY BLES
LONDON

© RUTH DAVIES, 1961

Printed in Great Britain by
Butler & Tanner, Ltd., Frome
for the publishers

GEOFFREY BLES LTD

52 DOUGHTY STREET, LONDON, W.C.1
33 YORK STREET, SYDNEY
531 LITTLE COLLINS STREET, MELBOURNE
200A ALBERT STREET, BRISBANE
CML BUILDING, KING WILLIAM STREET, ADELAIDE
WYNDHAM STREET, AUCKLAND
10 DYAS ROAD, DON MILLS, ONTARIO
P.O. BOX 8879, PALLSTATE HOUSE
51 COMMISSIONER STREET, JOHANNESBURG

First published 1961

To
THE PARISHIONERS OF PARHAM
AND WIGGONHOLT CUM GREATHAM

Note: My husband died before he could see this book through the press and in dedicating it to the people of his last parish his family and I are fulfilling what I am sure would have been his wish.

RUTH DAVIES

CONTENTS

CONTENTS

THERE is much to be yet written about the psychology of spiritual change, and especially of conversion and of the new birth which gives us our true eternity. For eternal life means more than immortality. We may hope for better light on the process when there are more cases, and more thorough, and more intelligent cases, of the new birth among people with the modern mind and the psychological insight.

P. T. FORSYTH
This Life and the Next

CHAPTER I

INTRODUCTION TO LIFE

I WAS BORN in Pontycymmer, one of the smaller mining towns in Glamorgan, South Wales, in 1889. The little place lies at the top of the Garw valley with the mountains rising steeply on three sides. In these grey mountains my life was formed. They were the cradle of my beginnings. Home was set in them and they were the limits of my world. They spoke to me of deep wonders in the heart of nature, of age and permanence, of a word I had not yet heard, and my heart was lifted up in expectation and longing. They awoke the sense of romantic adventure. During glamorous moon-lit nights, when the valley was clothed in unutterable beauty, I stood again and again wondering what lay beyond that bare skyline. Soft whispering of mystery and urgency echoed in my heart and in some dim and inexpressible way I had the feeling that great things were afoot.

I

The world into which I had come was one where an old tradition was losing its power and a new tradition was arising. Towards the close of the last century, in Wales, the long-maintained dominance of simple, stark religion in individual life was beginning to decline, and social reform was being given a religious significance. This was re-flected in the excitement of the appearance in 1900 of the first Independent Labour candidate in the Gower division, the steel workers' leader, John Hodge. His unsuccessful fight was more than political. It was possessed by religious fervour, for his chief supporters were all chapel men. My father was a very devoted member of the chapel, and was its musical conductor. He attended both Sunday services, also the Sunday School and the five o'clock prayer-meeting. He never missed the Monday prayer-meeting; he conducted the Band of Hope on Tuesday, the choir practice on Wednesday; and was present at the *Gyfeillach*, the testimony service, on Thursday, and on Saturday evening took part in the prayer-meeting for the Sunday services. He was an enthusiastic worker for the Labour candidate. In that election campaign he was made aware that something was missing from the chapel and its ceaseless round of religious activities. It was a premonitory sign, the early tint of autumn that was to descend upon the religious life of Wales. It was, at the same time, the first shoot that heralded the rise of secular politics. Thus I spent my boyhood—I was eleven at the time of the General Election—in the confluence of two traditions—the religious one at its ebb, and the social reform one at its initiation.

Let me be more explicit, for I do not mean that the struggle for social and economic change began only in the eighties; that would obviously be untrue. The whole of the nineteenth century in South Wales witnessed the waging of the class-struggle in its most naked brutality. Always miners were fighting in defence of their wretched living standards against the most ruthless of British employers—the South Wales coal owners. That South Wales coalfield was the most exposed and active front in the class-war of the century. The Welsh miners bore the fiercest brunt of the century's industrial battle throughout its whole course. But struggle never competed with religion for the spiritual allegiance of the miner. It was imposed upon him by sheer economic and physical necessity. The frenzied pursuit of world markets by the Welsh coal barons drove them mercilessly to cut down their costs of production, in which the chief item was wages. In the fierce competition for supremacy in coal, the Welsh owners were compelled to reduce to the minimum the amount of bread the miners and their children should consume. Against such attempts, the miners fought fiercely to avoid starvation. But their resistance in the economic field did not impinge upon their religious tradition. The religious life of the miner and his economic battle were two non-communicating spheres. The struggle against poverty made no inroad upon the vitality of religious faith. The chapel mediated the supreme spiritual values of life. The South Wales Miners' Federation was a weapon of earthly struggle.

Towards the close of the century a profound change was taking place. The economic struggle, which broadened out into general political agitation, began to acquire spiritual significance. It thus came into direct conflict with the religious tradition and began to eat into the vitals of chapel loyalties. As, for instance, when devoted chapel adherents would miss an occasional prayer-meeting for a political meeting—a portent! This was done with a certain amount of guilt-feeling, and not a little shamefacedly. That it was done at all was a sign that a new tide, destined to devitalize the chapels of Wales, had set in. It was a tide that carried away from the chapels a great deal of the brain and talent of Welsh youth. Hitherto, it had been a matter of course that children of gifts were set for the pulpit. The Nonconformist ministry was the open career for talent. Until the eighties, the Welsh pulpit had a monopoly of brains, passion and character. At the turn of the century, however, that monopoly began to disappear, and ability and character turned increasingly to politics and industrial leadership. This meant that the struggle for social and political change began to acquire a religious meaning. It became a competing field for the spiritual idealism of Welsh youth. God came to be equated with society—the working-class section of it in particular. One of the results was a sharp and deep conflict, which was reflected in the character and psychology of the individual.

Of course, there was a good objective reason for this

social and religious transition. In an era of change, religion appears deficient in social consciousness. So long as the foundations of society are secure, religion is far more concerned about individual relationships and ethical duties than social obligations. Throughout the whole of the nineteenth century, capitalist society was technically and socially progressive. Its industrial inventiveness stimulated the production of wealth and economic organization, and promoted the development of the political structure. Its basis was, therefore, secure. No social system whose foundations are solid can be seriously challenged, whatever its injustices and defects. Capitalist society in the nineteenth century, especially in South Wales, was cruel and savage beyond belief; its injustices were monstrous, but it did put history forward, so that it met no challenge, as a system, from church and chapel, for both preached a morality that was useful for the development of Capitalism. For instance, thrift and work were proclaimed the pre-eminent virtues—which, indeed, they were from a capitalist point of view. By means of thrift, the consumer learns to forgo present consumption in favour of capital accumulation, which serves to increase capacity to produce, and helps British industry to capture world markets. Work as a duty in itself was challenged by no one, and the employer himself set an example of labour, which he forced upon those dependent upon him. To what extent this is Christian is debatable. That it was socially progressive admits of no doubt. But, under Christian sanctions, social progress was achieved at the cost of enormously strengthening the acquisitive instinct which finally makes society itself impossible, as our divided Europe in the second decade of the new century demonstrates to all.

In the eighties, a slight tremor made itself felt in the foundations of our own capitalist society. The entry of a victorious Germany and a reunited America into the markets of the world checked the hitherto unmatched technical and social progress of Great Britain. Crises of over-production became intense and prolonged. Capitalism functioned with increasing difficulty. Consequently its morality came into question. The social movement that arose when I was born became a challenge to Capitalism as a system. Challenge to a social system demands a philosophy, an ideal, a spiritual valuation of man and life. In other words, the existence of a society cannot be questioned in the name of economics alone. Ultimately, the challenge must be in the name of religion, explicit or implicit. The inability of church and chapel to protest against Capitalism inevitably meant, in South Wales, that Socialism became a competitor with the Churches as an expression of religion, of Christianity. This was the unique and significant thing in the new social development. It witnessed to a defect in organized Christianity. It facilitated the fatal process of the secularization of religion, for the attempt to spiritualize politics led to the secularization of Christianity in the mind of a whole generation. And of this generation I am a microcosm. I was born into a process of inevitable frustration. On the one hand, I unconsciously inherited a failing tradition. On the other, I grew into manhood under the conscious influence of a new tradition that could not, by its very nature, meet the need that the old left unfulfilled. The religious tradition no longer fed the soul and satisfied its eternal hunger because of the emergence of social disintegration. The new tradition attempted to substitute for the soul's hunger a social satisfaction. The result was to imprison men in an exasperating contradiction.

This was the tragedy of my generation, through which I have lived to the bitter, bitter death. I started life in the rosy illusion which was destined to inflict upon us all the most cruel suffering. Our final barque was set on lively waters which concealed a whirlpool, in which we were condemned to eddy around until sucked into its despairing depths. The defeat and frustration of my generation I have shared in fullest measure. In a very real sense, I am representative of a whole disastrous world; and because frustration has not been the final word with me I venture to give my story. The futilities and defeats of over half a lifetime have been swallowed up in splendid victory. But not without wounds whose scars remain. But transcendence of the contradiction of the generation into which I was born is not an individual, temperamental oddity. On the contrary, it is the most common experience, which countless numbers of men and women have discovered through many earlier generations in the great historic Faith in Jesus Christ. The Faith which saves an individual is no less able to save a generation and a world.

2

Let me give now the essential, preliminary facts.

I spent the first eight years of my life in my birth-place, Pontycymmer; then my parents moved to Clydach-on-Tawe, a small town five miles up the Swansea valley, in which the two industries were coal-mining and tinplate. My father was appointed choirmaster, at a small salary, in the Welsh Independent Chapel. We lived next door to the chapel. I have a lively memory of that house. All the living accommodation was on the ground floor, the upstairs being one large room, which was the property of the Rechabites' Friendly Society and was used as a meeting-hall. At one end, in the centre, was the platform with a reading-desk. How often did I steal up to that room, and, mounting the platform, orate to that empty hall, which my imagination peopled with a packed and thrilled audience! It was a gorgeous luxury. Up in that room, alone, I was the prince of preachers.

Our daydreams take their material from our environment. I was a preacher in the upper room because my home was intensely religious. My mother was a woman of outstanding character, a magnificent Christian, to whom religion was a constant, living reality, penetrating every fibre of her being. Our home-life took its colour from her. In those formative years, it was her vital spirit that influenced me most.

In our daily family life there were family prayers. Every night before going to bed, which for a youngster was late, my father read a portion of scripture and my mother offered the prayer. I never forget the fervour with which she prayed. We were four children, of whom I was the youngest. We all had to kneel, which I often found irksome, but something of eternity came to me through those prayers. Every night I had to be present for family worship; for absence meant the strap, fear of which exercised greater compulsion than the most absorbing games. Contrary to many of the generalizations of the new psychology, I declare that I had never any emotion of hatred for prayers then or later. I accepted them as a fact.

My mother taught me the catechism from a little work by Dr. Thomas Charles, which exercised a profound influence in Welsh religious life for many years. It was entitled *Rhodd Mam* (Mother's Gift). In the most desperate agony of my later life, it was the memory of my mother's teaching from that little book that overwhelmed me. She inculcated Christian dogma by question and answer—and no nonsense. The psychologists would say that she rammed dogma down my throat. And she did—good and hard. Its value and significance did not materialize until I was approaching fifty, as I shall tell the reader in the proper place.

I had to attend all the chapel services with my father, sitting with him behind the pulpit, in front of the organ, from which place he would direct the choir. I had a full, central view of the congregation, which provided ample interest and excitement. Nearly every week-night was occupied with religious activities of one sort or another from which I extracted my own compensations, for during the prayer-meeting I indulged in day-dreaming, undisturbed.

Thus religion was dominant in my early childhood. So in its way was culture.

Both my father and mother were uneducated, but highly cultured people, for they had a passionate interest in ideas. Yet neither had had even an elementary school education. My father once told me that one of his earliest recollections was of being carried on his father's back down to the coal-pit, when he was about seven or eight years old. Both parents learned to read Welsh, which was their only language until many years later. My mother could not speak a word of English till long after her fiftieth birthday, when she learnt to read it as well. And she read to some purpose—in theology. She then devoured all my theological text-books. Both father and mother were gifted and studious in their different ways. Father was a poet and musician. He wrote some fine Welsh poetry and composed a great number of anthems and hymn-tunes. He also composed a cantata performed with gusto by the chapel choir.

Theology was the main intellectual pursuit of both my parents. Being next door to the chapel, our home became a central meeting-place for the active members of the chapel from the minister downwards. Conversation was invariably about things that mattered, and ideas were the staple of intercourse. Without knowing it, I breathed a strong, stimulating intellectual atmosphere. In later years I realized what a great advantage I had enjoyed. It has been my lot to know at different times wealthy, polished and educated families amongst whom argument about great ideas was bad form. An entirely different and better start was mine. In my home-life, it was ideas that mattered. By their intellectual intensity my parents created in me a zest for ideas which gave direction to my life.

This was the environment in which my boyhood was spent: religion and culture were daily bread. I was encouraged to read and study. My father impressed upon me, when I was a lad of nine or ten, how important a thing was

education. He also insisted that I should learn to play some
musical instrument. Out of scanty pennies, music-lessons
were paid for. Starting with great enthusiasm, I soon tired,
however, and gave up the task, which indicated a deep
defect in my character, a defect that persisted, often with the
gravest consequences. Meanwhile, my home did for me as
a boy what the University is supposed to do, according to
Newman, for youth—it awoke and encouraged a love of
ideas for their own sake. And that advantage outweighed
most of the handicaps under which I lived, handicaps neither few nor light.

After about three or four years in Clydach, my father
obtained a job as lampman in a colliery in Maesteg, a mining
town of about 30,000 population, nine miles from Bridgend,
and twenty-eight from Cardiff. In due course, we moved to
Maesteg, which proved to be a momentous change, for there
I became a chapel member, obtained my first job (appren-
tice-boy in a grocer's shop) fell in love, became politically
conscious and active, and preached my first sermon, the
text of which was "Flee youthful lusts". These youthful
lusts must have exercised a great fascination for me. Or
was it the self-righteous, priggish morality of one who
denounces sins that do not happen to tempt him? How
aware I am now of the insufferable conceit and egotism of
my youth, and how unaware, no doubt, I am of my present
conceit and vanity! Those years of boyhood and youth were
hard, bitter years of poverty, in which circumstances ordained, much against my will, that I should, for a time, be
the sole breadwinner of the family. Poverty was the grim
discipline used by Providence to ends I knew not of.

CHAPTER II

THE SCHOOL OF POVERTY

M<small>Y EARLY CHILDHOOD</small>, lived in extreme poverty, was made endurable by my mother's strength of character, not my own. In some way or other she managed to endow the poverty of the home with dignity. Yet no amount of camouflage and desperate managing could hide the fact that I was conscious of the difference between the clothes I wore and those of my playmates and schoolfellows. This early poverty bred in me a sense of revolt. As early as I can remember, I was possessed by an inner protest against the lack of necessities. Why couldn't I have a new suit like other boys? Why should I be condemned to wear clothes made out of my father's or brother's old wear? Other boys had their pennies to spend on sweets each week. I had to share my halfpenny with my sister. When the annual fair was held with its merry-go-rounds, stalls and side-shows, my coppers were miserable compared with the silver coins in the hands of other boys. I felt deprived and discontented. I had a grudge.

Having a grudge fostered my native pride and egotism. In later life, the fact of this childhood's poverty enabled me to justify myself in holding on to self-will and pride. It formed in me the habit of shifting responsibility for the failure and disasters of life on to other shoulders. My poverty violated the first principle of a really sound education, which, according to Kierkegaard, is to allow the soul to be moulded by responsibility. My soul was moulded by irresponsibility. It was my father's fault, or somebody's fault, that I had only a halfpenny a week. By the time I reached manhood, I had come to assume that the blame always lay somewhere else—never with myself. I had to pass through an insanity of suffering before I realized the fundamental moral law of personal responsibility.

It was early poverty that encouraged the basic weakness in my character to be exhibited chiefly in my attitude to money. I never consciously reasoned in this way, of course. But I developed a violent distaste for being without money, so violent indeed that a sense of obligation hardly existed where money was concerned. It is a commonplace that hard-earned money teaches one its value and makes one careful in the use of it, but that most certainly was not true with me. On the contrary, extreme lack of money engendered a spirit of recklessness. I got the habit of borrowing money, always with the intention of paying it back, but actually indifferent to whether I did so or not. I lent when I had it; when I did not have it, I even borrowed to lend, which sometimes led me into serious difficulties. The fact is, I never learned to value money consciously—a fatal defect, especially in one who was to go into the ministry. I write this quite objectively, because I now feel an entirely different attitude to money, which is one of the ethical transformations in my life.

I thus carried from childhood to manhood, with all its fatal consequences, a grudge against society which I later rationalized in a passionate zeal for socialism, and an un-awareness of basic personal responsibility, which especially came to operate in money matters.

I

Before I was born, my father suffered a serious injury down the pit. His back was broken by a fall of rock. For nearly ten years he was unable to do a stroke of work. That was in the days when there was no employers' liability, and throughout all those years of enforced idleness, my father received not one penny in compensation, though he never again could work as a miner. From a tall, strong, upright figure, he was transformed into a hunchback, never able completely to dress himself. What a purgatory he had to suffer, and what a martyrdom had my mother to endure!

When the accident happened, there were three children. I, soon after, made a fourth. Four growing children, strong and healthy; four mouths to feed and four pairs of feet to be shod. That was the problem facing my mother. And in the solution of it the four children had their part to play. Circumstances left no room for the sentimentalities. It was a grim struggle. And my mother's spirit pulled us through.

Two things she did to meet the situation: she kept lodgers, three of them, and she had a little shop of sweets and fruit. A St. Teresa behind a counter! My brother went down the pit at thirteen, and my elder sister did day work as a domestic servant. My younger sister and I helped in the shop. There was a cast-iron law about the fruit and sweets, for, as far as we were concerned, they were non-consumable commodities. Indeed, without that law, any profits on the enterprise would have been literally eaten up. I came to have the same regard for the delectables of the shop as a well-trained sheep dog develops for his master's sheep—untouchable!

In an earlier day in Glamorgan, ground-floor rooms in working-class houses had stone floors, and it was the custom for housewives to sprinkle sand over them at the week-end. The stone floor would be scrubbed to the brightness of marble, for cleanliness was next to godliness, and then the glory would be dimmed by dirty brown sand. What a saturnalia the germs enjoyed each week-end! It was through this unhygienic custom that I first entered the ranks of the world's workers.

We sold the sand at the price of one penny per bucket, the customer supplying the bucket. On the Saturday morning, round about 6 a.m., I had to go to the railway station with a hired horse and cart to bring a load of sand to the shop. There it was tipped out. I then had to call at our customers' houses, one by one, to ask for the buckets, return to the shop, fill the buckets with sand and take them back to the customer, each for one penny. The utter idiocy of it is what impresses me now. From early morning till late afternoon to endure all that labour to spread dirt! An eloquent commentary on the civilization of the nineties! But I cannot recall any resentment. I suppose I must occasionally have felt unwilling to do the work, when I saw other boys at play, but that I cannot remember. Indeed I probably enjoyed it, for driving a horse was a great adventure.

That was only part of my work.

During the week, I had to sell kippers from door to door, before going to school at nine o'clock. I was out of bed at seven each morning, except Monday. I set off with a basket of kippers, every one of which I sold, after which I returned for a hasty breakfast. Then I went to school. It was in such circumstances that I formed the habit of gobbling food, which I do to this day. In spite of the dire warnings I have often received, no ill consequences have accrued. I suppose God gave me a first-class stomach, for I can eat anything, and in double-quick time, and have never suffered the faintest trace of indigestion.

This was the first phase of my life covering the period during which I lived in my birthplace, Pontycymmer. In later life I underwent a course of psycho-analysis in which the brilliant analyst did his best to get me to recall other memories of that period, but failed. My subconscious must have been an ocean of sand packed with kippers.

2

When we moved to Clydach-on-Tawe, the struggle for existence became less severe. My father, as well as becoming choirmaster at the Independent Chapel, started work as a check-weigher at a small pit. His wages from the two occupations did not exceed two pounds a week. In addition, there were my brother's earnings, round about a pound a week. Three pounds per week was wealth, compared with our situation at Pontycymmer, but more had to be done with it, and three pounds for six people did not run to affluence.

I had two occupations throughout these years, one of which was significant for its revelation of a grave temperamental weakness, which cursed my character until very recently, which no amount of effort or determination on my part has affected in the slightest. The first was that of butcher's errand-boy on Saturdays. Starting at 9 a.m., I ran errands until seven or eight at night, for which I received one shilling in cash and two meals, which then was good pay. I was conscious of being somebody when I handed the shilling over to my mother on Saturday night. I glowed with pride. I was a wage-earner. I knew nothing then of the exploitation in labour processes. My feeling was that of someone playing a part, and making a contribution, however little, which had its value. I believe it helped to engender a certain toughness at the core, which enabled me in later life to hang on in desperate circumstances. At the age of nine or ten, I was somebody, for I was earning a shilling a week. Later on in the same Welsh valleys, as elsewhere, a youth of twenty felt himself to be nobody, because he had never earned a penny in his life. It is the man who is made aware of being nobody who deludes himself—and destroys civilization by his delusion that he can become a somebody by handing himself over body and soul to a leader of a party. Whatever disintegrating effect later experience had upon me, I started with some iron in my consciousness. It was pride. But pride with iron in it is better, even for the Kingdom of God, than a character made of jelly.

My second occupation was that of newspaper boy, which I mention for a special reason. After school hours I delivered the evening paper, *The Cambrian News*, to a number of houses for a few coppers a night. But I had to cover a great deal of ground. In the course of an evening's delivery I would walk about four or five miles. One incident, which has a significance all its own, stands out.

One winter evening, when I was about half way on my round, I suddenly felt I did not want to do this work any more. The revulsion was so strong that it obsessed my whole being. It paralysed my will. What was to be done? There I was, with several dozens of papers which I was determined not to deliver. Why? I don't know. The force of my feeling blotted out all consequences. That people would be expecting their evening sheet; that the news-agent would be wondering what had happened at my non-return; and that he would be angry. None of these things deflected me. I was not going to deliver any more papers. But what to do with them? How to explain matters at home?

I solved the problem by pretending to be ill. I sat down in the street with my bundle beside me, and holding my stomach with both hands, I groaned and cried. Before long I believed I was really ill. I have always been able to believe my own lies for a while. I soon gathered a little crowd around me, and became the object of general sympathy. A kindly soul took the papers back to the shop, and another took me home and explained matters to my mother who, with anxiety and promptitude, put me to bed—a thing I had not bargained for. In this distant incident of my boyhood emerged the fundamental problem of my life, the solution of which lay beyond my power. I want to emphasize that fact. The same situation, in different terms, of course, recurred many times. Each time I was helpless. I was seized by a sudden, irresistible revulsion against doing what I knew should be done. I did not do it. Instead, I lied; I pretended; I deceived myself; I rationalized. I knew what I *ought* to do. But I could not do it. That I did not admit my inability was my sin and tragedy. I believed in my own lie. In the affair of the newspapers, I felt that my employer was unfair, that he expected too much of me, and that I really was ill. And so through all my life, until I was made a new man, I never admitted to myself the simple truth. I never cried:

> *"Oh! That a power would arise in me*
> *That the man I am may cease to be."*

I carefully screened "the man I am" from exposure.

This experience has been repeated in my life in a sort of rhythm which made for a distressing instability of character. I would enjoy a period, more or less prolonged, of accord with my work and environment, when I would carry out the duties of my situation whatever they happened to be: all was well, and I was happy. My native optimism rode the seas of circumstance serenely. But then would come—suddenly, unaccountably—revulsion and disgust; and I was helpless. Duties were neglected, difficulties accumulated, until at last I was consumed by melancholy and despair; I shunned society and suffered acutely. I got the reputation of being unstable—a reputation fully merited. I never called it that. I persuaded myself of all sorts of abysmally silly and unreal things. At one time, for instance, when I was under the influence of Jacob Kraemer, the Jewish artist, I persuaded myself that I had the artistic temperament, and became a hero to myself, a lonely, magnificent hero. My pride drove down a bit deeper. I was really an artist. My medium was preaching. What a pathetic business it was! In course of time, I worked back to enjoyment of my work. Thus life was a see-saw. I became a creature of the dark—driven by necessity. It began when consciously that night I sat down in the street with my papers undelivered.

3

It was during my life in Clydach that there awoke in me two interests that were to influence considerably my intellectual development. These were music and history.

As I have already indicated, my father had no mean

musical talent. As choirmaster of the chapel, he was responsible for many musical activities, so that I lived in an atmosphere of music. Hardly a night passed that he did not have somebody at home for musical tuition of some kind. My two sisters and brother were gifted with good voices. My younger sister had the making of a first-rate soprano; my elder sister had a beautiful contralto voice; and my brother was a tenor and sang for a while in the Moody Manners Opera Company. I was the only one without a singing voice. That did not mean I was exempt from instruction.

My father had the idea that no one could be really educated without a knowledge and appreciation of music and he did his best to inculcate in his children a deep love of it. He taught me the rudiments of tonic sol-fa, which, to this day, I can read more easily than staff notation. A score written in sol-fa I can hear with my eyes. I have an idea of the harmony from reading it. But my father was not really a good teacher. He was too impatient. The need for repeated or varied explanations made him angry, and then my brain ceased to function. But he pulled me through the examinations of the Tonic Sol-Fa College. He also taught me to appreciate vocal music—good music, too. I quite early knew the difference, not only between good and bad singing, but also between good and bad music. I was constantly listening to Bach, Handel, Mozart, Mendelssohn and Schubert—oratorios, cantatas and masses.

I had to learn an instrument. I chose the violin. In spite of poverty, money was found to pay for lessons. As my younger sister and brother had voice training, a goodly proportion of the family income must have been spent on music. I never became really proficient, however, though I played in different orchestras at different times, and even played first violin. What it did for me chiefly was to create an ear for tone, which is an indispensable minimum for the appreciation especially of chamber and orchestral music.

My interest in history was awakened by one of my schoolteachers, John Davies. In his way he was a genius. I have been privileged to listen to many first-rate historians, as for example, Professor Richard Lodge lecturing on European History at Edinburgh. But my elementary teacher had a quality other teachers lacked. If the function of a teacher is to create in his pupils an independent passion for know-ledge, then John Davies was a true educator, one of the best I have known. His history lessons created an un-quenchable thirst and I read voraciously whatever I could get hold of. Before I was twelve I had read Macaulay's *History of England*. To this day I recall the painful excitement with which I followed the trial of the seven bishops.

My teacher had the knack of making his students realize that history was an affair of real human beings. Even when he talked about kings and queens, he showed them to be men and women. That was his secret. He made the past contemporary.

He created in me, too, a specific historical interest that I have never lost, to which from time to time I have paid considerable attention, military strategy and tactics. I have studied with a good deal of fascination, if not always with understanding, the development of war, which concen-trates the story of technical progress. Scientific invention is perfected by war, and for war—a fact of profound moral significance. War has a dialectic peculiarity of its own. Man's creative faculty finds its greatest stimulus in the service of destruction, which symbolizes some profound futility and contradiction in human effort.

Here, then, I had from my father and my school-teacher two essential elements of a liberal education—music and history. I got them in the most unpromising circumstances. My school days were spent in the age of big classes—and no theories. The reader must not interpret this as a condemna-tion of small classes and educational experimentation. My aim is to show what we are in danger of underestimating; namely, that personality can rise above circumstances. A class of sixty boys and girls could not prevent my teacher from giving his children a sound educational foundation.

Let me point out that the Welsh Nonconformity in which I was reared did not make for narrowness and fanaticism of mind as so many of the frustrated, embittered critics of my generation have maintained. Today we are living upon the capital of those same "tin Bethels", and when that gives out (as it is now doing) the futility and leanness of our contemporary life will become more obvious and disastrous. It is true that our fathers, in Wales, taught us a religion of cast-iron dogma, which, according to all the theories, should have made us obscurantists, inhabiting a very small world. But it did not. In some mysterious way we became freemen of a spacious world. Along beside the narrow dogma went a broad culture. What happened to me demonstrates that fact clearly. Can anything promote a wider interest than history? And history led to politics, which, in turn, opened the door on many intellectual horizons. And music. It fed the spirit as an instrument of perception, as an organ of knowledge. It made for inner refinement. We had few of the graces and polish of manners, characteristic of an affluent and secure society, but music gave us something better. It created in us a fastidiousness of moral as well as literary taste. It gave us a sense of the necessary relation between content and form. I very much doubt whether, fundamentally, Eton or Harrow would have given me a better start, educationally, than the "tin Bethel", the elementary council school, and my home.

There was another factor in my education of immense importance—the Bible.

Bible-reading was an institution of Welsh family life. People knew their Bible. It was a layman's book. The almost complete absence of Bible-reading in the family life of today is rapidly making the Bible a one-man book—that is, the minister's. It is becoming the preserve of a profession. That part of the essence of Roman Catholicism is thus occupying

—unobserved—the citadels of Protestantism. The neglect of
the Bible by the layman is preparing a rich harvest for Rome,
to say nothing of the present-day impoverishment of preaching. Great preaching cannot thrive on the Biblical ignorance of the layman. That is now the position. As long ago
as 1939, only 8 per cent. of the candidates for the Central
Welsh Board certificate passed in scripture, as I was informed by my friend, Professor Vernon Lewis of Brecon,
one of the examiners.

A very different state of things obtained in my childhood.
Parents undertook the responsibility of encouraging their
children to read the Bible, and set the example by reading it
themselves. I still see my father, after his return from work,
having had his bath and dinner, sitting down in the fireside
armchair with the Bible on his knees. My mother was even
a more assiduous reader than he. She was the greatest Bible
student I have ever known. I once caused offence at a meeting of theologians when I said that my mother's insight
into the Bible, minus every shred of scholarship, was deeper
and profounder than that of any contemporary theologian,
with the exception of Karl Barth. What a pity those two
never met! The greatest thing about Barth is not his scholarship, which is no great shakes, but his prophetic insight into
the Bible. Well, that is exactly what my mother had. She
used to meet me with excitement on my return from school
some days because she had discovered a new meaning to
a chapter she had been studying. I had to learn several verses
to recite twice a week—once in the prayer-meeting and at
the Sunday evening service, "*yr ail gwydd*", the second meeting. And they had to be different each time. At special services during the year, I had to recite whole psalms and
chapters. I thus learnt a good deal of the Bible.

My parents also encouraged me—bribed me shall I say?—
to read the Bible by promising me a shilling (a fabulous
sum) for reading it through in a year. Of course, whole
stretches of it meant absolutely nothing to me, but a good

deal of it did. I found the stories of Genesis and Exodus, Judges, Kings and Chronicles fascinating. They lived. I was involved in the story of Joseph and his brothers. Indeed, I did not need the stimulus of the shilling to read the stories. But the bargain was that I was to read the whole, which I did several times in both Welsh and English. And I defy any child of ordinary intelligence to read the Bible constantly (in the Authorized Version) without acquiring a genuine literary taste, a sense of style, and at least a feeling for the beauty of words. Before I was twelve I had developed an appreciation of good prose, and the Bible created in me a zest for literature. I went direct from the Bible to Charles Lamb, Hazlitt and Ruskin. How I came to these writers I forget, but I distinctly remember, during the Clydach days, reading paper-covered copies of Lamb's and Hazlitt's Essays, and Ruskin's *Crown of Wild Olive*. Lamb's "Confessions of a Drunkard" made a vivid impression on me—for I happened to be reading, at the same time, a book entitled *Buy Your Own Cherries*, a Temperance classic of those days. It was on the Bible that my literary taste was formed.

4

This Clydach phase came to an end somewhere about 1900–1901. It had been an exciting, happy time—and one immediately significant for my spiritual and intellectual development. Three great things had happened.

First, the basic problem of my whole life had formulated itself—a profound consciousness of impotence which I carefully refused to recognize and admit. What a difference it might have made had some angel enabled me, that night of the newspapers incident, to make a clean breast of my lying and pretence! But as I have hinted and shall later describe, I began a career of self-deception, by means of which I endeavoured to maintain a false optimism about myself, my pride, my egotism. Subsequent knowledge and education merely deepened that self-deception and enlarged my pride, until at last it involved me in ruin and despair. In 1898, I cast aside only a bundle of halfpenny papers. "It was in a puddle that I learnt how to sink."

Second, there were laid down some of the main lines along which my intellectual interests were to develop—History, Music and Religion: a wonderful trinity! Today, history is possibly my deepest intellectual passion, not as a mere record or narrative, rather as a philosophy of human destiny. I make no pretence whatever to scholarship, but I have read widely and deeply in European history, at least.

My love of music, which my father first inculcated in those far-off days, has also continued to grow in spite of the fact that I have completely neglected it for long periods. For instance, during my first year in London (about which I shall have a good deal to say later on), when I could not earn a penny, I sold part of my library in order to buy a season ticket for the Promenade Concerts, and did not miss a single concert. I then had to walk from Palmers Green to Queen's Hall and back again after the concert, each night, for pennies were too scarce for bus fares. Oh! Those nights with their ache and loneliness! There must have been some deep hunger in my soul for music. It began in Clydach when I was nine or ten years of age, when hymns in the minor key made me weep. Indeed, music has brought me great suffering. There are some works to which I can hardly bear to listen, particularly the second part of Tchaikovsky's Swan Lake ballet music. But Tchaikovsky's is supremely the music of man unredeemed, his despair and frustration.

The third thing that happened to me in this Clydach phase was the awakening of romance, a divinely ecstatic experience. It was pure joy. It had none of the pain of adolescent and adult passion. It was a fleeting, momentary dawn which dissolved, not into day with its inevitable shadow and oppression, but into nothingness: an experience that bore no congruity to its objective stimulus. It happened one Christmas night, when a girl many years my senior unexpectedly kissed me under the mistletoe— and then vanished. It was pure ecstasy. If I have ever had a perfect experience, that was it. I was not more than twelve years old. It was as though body spontaneously became spirit, and for a moment my perceptions became ethereal.

I mention it here because of its spiritual significance. I took not the slightest interest in the girl. It did not occur to me to go in search of her. I didn't even connect the kiss with the mistletoe. But it gave me, I believe, a hint of perfection, an idea of the sexes before the Fall. I think it was from that experience that the intimation awakened in my conscious- ness that spirit is a greater factor in sex than the physical. I should be a miserable humbug were I to try to persuade the reader that that has been my predominating experience. It has not.

In 1900 or 1901, calamity fell upon our household. The pit at which my father worked closed down, and he became unemployed. Owing to his physical disability he could per- form no heavy labour. His occupation had to be very light employment. None could be found in the district. Days of hardship returned. At length, my father was offered the post of underground lampman at a colliery in Maesteg, the mana- ger of which was an old friend. So we moved there. For me it meant a great deal. I had just won a scholarship for the county school at Ystalyfera and I was destined not to enjoy it.

So to Maesteg we went, my parents, brother, two sisters —and the cat. I remember the cat. We had the devil's own time with it. It got out of its bag and we had the greatest difficulty in recapturing and pacifying it. But we arrived safe at last in our new home, which was to be my world for the next twelve or thirteen years.

CHAPTER III

GREEK AND COAL

MAESTEG IS ONE of the pleasantest coal-valleys of Glamorgan. It is a wide valley, and the collieries are situated away in the mountains, so that the town hardly wears the aspect of a colliery district, as do the Rhondda, the Garw and Monmouthshire valleys. It is surrounded by delightful scenery and within eight miles of the sea. Thus I escaped a good deal of the sordidness and drabness characteristic of so many colliery areas. This unspoilt beauty of country developed my early sense of natural beauty, a matter of great significance, for it was the source from which a genuine artistic interest sprang in later life. Thus it made its contribution to my education. Indeed, I have been a most fortunate man, for I have touched life at so many points and my founts of inspiration have been many. Through sheer good luck, or by the hand of Providence, I was educationally reared in the Humanities—Music, Literature, History, Religion, Philosophy and Art. Had I been an earl's son, smothered with opportunities, I could not have acquired greater or deeper interests. And Maesteg, to which economic change had taken my parents, had mountain, woodland and sea, which aroused in me the deepest sense of beauty and wonder.

I

But there was very little of aesthetics in the immediate circumstances. After a few months as an apprentice in a grocer's shop—Lipton's—which I *loathed*, I got a job, much against the wishes of my mother, down the pit. My mother, like all Welsh mothers, wanted to keep me away from coalmining. But I hated the grocery trade. I rebelled against the long hours; for, except one half-day a week, I was working from 8.30 a.m. till 8.0 p.m. every night—except on Saturdays when it was 11.30 or 12.0 p.m. For another thing, I sensed a snobbishness in the atmosphere of the shop. Since most of the things I have to say about myself in this narrative are not flattering, let me say that I am not a snob. I never have been a snob, except possibly an inverted one, for I used to take pride in the fact that I was of working-class origin. When middle-class people expressed surprise and admiration at the fact that I had worked in a colliery, I actually purred. I never tried to hide the fact. On the contrary, I advertised it blatantly. But I find it difficult to refrain from contempt when I meet people who think in terms of "lower orders" and "good families". During my boyhood days in Maesteg, shop assistants considered themselves a cut above colliers. My fellow assistants oozed snobbery from every pore, and I reacted violently. I felt alien to such thoughts and I had not been in the shop a week before I was utterly sick of it. The thought arose and grew that I should "chuck" it and go down the pit. It took me some weeks to gain my mother's consent, but at length my father approached the manager of the pit where he worked, and got me a job. It was a thrilling day when I "signed on".

It was still more thrilling when I went to my first day's work at 7 a.m. That is, I had to be down the pit by that time. I was out of bed at 5.30. Whilst I was excited, I was also afraid. I gripped hard the handrail in the cage that lowered the men to the pit-bottom. My first job was "door-boy". I had to shut and open the ventilation doors to the passage of horse-drawn trams of coal. At first, it was lonely and eerie in the dark. I was scared of the rats and black-beetles—huge, horrible things. I never really got used to them, though, of course, the shrinking fear passed in time.

My first wages were two shillings a day. I started as a miner before the passing of the Eight-Hour Day. During the winter I saw daylight only twice a week. It was dark when I went down the pit in the morning, and dark when I came up at night. On Saturdays, however, we finished at midday—and that was compensation for a good deal.

Except for two breaks, one of two years and another of seven months, I worked as a miner for ten years, during which time I followed several occupations. After my first job as "door-boy", I worked as a labourer, as repairer's assistant and as coal-hewer. Coal-mining is no picnic. At best the work is hard and exhausting. I knew what it was to cut and load my six and seven tons of coal a day. I also knew what it was to work even harder than that and cut barely a ton a day owing to the nature of the ground and hardness of the seam. Sometimes, I arrived home too tired to have a bath. Often my mother took off my heavy working boots and lay me down on the sofa until I had rested. But it was a tiredness from which one soon recovered. I enjoyed marvellous health. My vitality was inexhaustible. After a hard day's work, I worked hard at recreation. There were meetings of various kinds—trade-union lodge meetings, chapel meetings, lectures, literary and debating gatherings, local *eisteddfods*, and so forth. Then a few hours' reading. It was a life brimful of activity and excitement.

On the whole, I think I can truthfully say that I enjoyed my work in the pit. If necessity compelled me, even now at this late time in my life, to choose how to earn my living by manual work, I should choose coal-mining in preference to any other, for all its hardship. Of course, I worked before the days of the conveyor belt and the pneumatic pick, which, I am told, make coal-mining today a little hell, besides robbing a man of his sense of craft. I certainly felt a pride in my work. Skill meant a great deal, involving one's own life as well as the lives of others. A badly timbered roof for instance, might mean a fall of rock, bringing death.

Coal-mining taught me the priceless value of *camaraderie*, of standing in with one's fellow-workers. I was always a good trade-unionist. When I drew my first week's wages

I joined the Federation. I got that from my father who, though never active, was always a staunch member of the union. I learnt the value of co-operation in the hard class-struggle of the South Wales coalfield. That is one reason why I have so little patience with ministers of religion when they indulge, as many of them do, in sentimentality about the wickedness of class-struggle. As though class-struggle were the personal luxury of the worker, and not a grim necessity imposed upon him by capitalism!

2

About the year 1903 or 1904 there occurred an event which considerably influenced my immediate future. That was the great Welsh Revival in which my younger sister, Annie Davies, as she then was, played a great part.

For about a year the revival, under the leadership of Evan Roberts, swept Wales from end to end. My recollection of it is clear and undimmed. It was the swan-song of the old religious tradition in Wales. Summer is at its richest just before it passes into autumn, and Spengler has observed the same thing about civilizations. They enjoy their bloom as they begin to decay. The revival was certainly a remarkable phenomenon, the consumptive's flush of death. A mighty mass-emotion possessed a whole people. Chapels were filled to over-flowing every night of the week for nearly a whole year, and men and women were converted by the thousand. The whole thing was spontaneous. At my home all the chapels held their prayer-meetings every night, without any leadership. People just prayed and sang hymns, and in that atmosphere men broke down. The so-called "bad" characters of the town—drunkards, rabbit-poachers, wasters, non-chapel goers—were converted in hundreds. That was happening all over Wales. I am not attempting any critical estimate or appreciation of the Revival, simply describing it in so far as it affected me in my life and prospects. Like all human happenings it was a mixture of elements. It certainly was, to some extent, a movement from God. Many lives were changed for good—and permanently.

One Saturday afternoon when I returned from work, my mother met me at the gate, holding a letter in her hand. She was very excited. My sister had been converted and was accompanying Evan Roberts on his missions at different places, as a singing evangelist. That certainly impressed me, in spite of the scepticism that a brother feels about his sister. She and Evan Roberts were appearing that very evening at a place called Abergwynfi, some five or six miles away, and I was to accompany my mother to the meeting. Well! I went and nothing happened! I was rather bewildered. My mother was very moved. I heard Evan Roberts speak and my sister sing, and scores of people were converted. I was not one of them.

In due course, Evan Roberts came to Maesteg and stayed at my home. He was a man of great power and charm, and he impressed me immensely. I remember being moved at one of his Maesteg meetings. I cannot recall now how or when I was "converted", but it was certainly after one of his visits. That is to say, at some meeting or other, I walked up to the front pew, the "*set fawr*" and publicly announced, along with others, that I was "saved". For a considerable time I attended nightly prayer-meetings, offered prayer myself, and button-holed people urging them to confess their sins. One important consequence was that I decided to go in for the ministry.

My conversion, such as it was, did not as far as I can remember make much, if any, ethical difference to me. It intensified me emotionally and made me say prayers. I read the Bible assiduously. I carried a pocket New Testament to work. I became "religious". I developed theological zealotry of the Fundamentalist kind. And I started preaching. But I am quite certain that there was no depth in the experience. I simply reflected my environment.

During these Revival days, my home was a prolonged prayer-meeting or religious gathering. People came, literally, from all over the world to our home to meet the parents of the famous young girl evangelist, as my sister had become. With few exceptions, of whom the Rev. Keri Evans professor of philosophy at the Presbyterian College, Carmarthen, was one, they were a fanatical crowd. Pentecostals mostly, Bible literalists, and such people. I took my cue and colour from them.

I have been in sufficient bitter waters since that time to believe that I must have been intolerably priggish and self-righteous. I told my father that he was not "saved". There was an unholy row. The way he went for me was certainly not that of a saint. But the impertinence! I was about fifteen years of age, certain I was saved, and still more certain that my father and others of my acquaintance were not saved.

It was on this foundation that I felt a "call" to preach. Not a very solid one as subsequent events proved only too quickly. I had become a chapel member at Zoar, the Welsh Independent Chapel, in which my parents were members. Shortly after, it was decided to form a new English Congregational Church, for which purpose a few members from different Welsh Chapels created a nucleus. I was one of the foundation members of this Bethlehem English Congregational Church, where I spent many happy times and made one lasting friendship. I was a leading light in that little church, except for those periods when my light went out, as it did occasionally; for the experience I have described in connection with my work as newsboy repeated itself in my relation to the church. One day I suddenly felt a distaste for the services and for everything connected with the church and stayed away entirely. I had a Sunday School class and played the violin at the services, for we had an orchestra composed of the organist and myself, but when my demon visited me I completely ignored these responsibilities. This happened more than once.

Otherwise I was active in all sorts of ways. I preached and read papers at the debating society. In due course, the church recommended me for the ministry. And it was decided that I should enter a preparatory school to prepare for the entrance examination to New College, London. But long before that happened, my weakness and instability, seconded by the serious illness of my father, ordained a very different sequence of events.

3

At the age of sixteen, or thereabouts, I went back to school again, to Old College School, Carmarthen, of which the Rev. Joseph Harry was proprietor and master. He had over a hundred pupils, most of them preparing for the ministry. In the task of teaching these budding theologians he had the help of one assistant, the Rev. J. B. Thomas. We were drilled in the rudiments of classics, mathematics, English, history, and a science. I tried to learn chemistry and geography.

I was there with the belief that I had a vocation for the ministry, but it had no depth. I was like the seeds in the parable which, without soil, sprang up and died. In the atmosphere of the school my ideas rapidly dissolved. That is, my Pentecostalism, my Biblical literalism, just vanished.

This return to school meant considerable effort and sacrifice on my parents' part. Not only was there the loss of my earnings, there was the expense of my maintenance. It may sound incredible, but I lived on ten shillings a week, which I received from home. I supplemented this with occasional preaching fees from the country chapels round about Carmarthen. School fees amounted to twenty-five shillings per term, to which must be added the cost of books. Altogether I had to live a spartan existence.

Shortly after I had settled in Carmarthen, I met a Unitarian student, who so greatly influenced me that I ultimately went into lodgings with him. His beliefs and arguments acted upon my emotional theology like acid. He was many years my senior and had read more than I. Before I knew where I was, I had become a Unitarian, which caused my parents—my mother particularly—great distress. To the passionate Protestantism of South Wales Nonconformity in those days, Unitarianism was equivalent to leprosy. Unitarians were a race apart. In the mining valleys they hardly existed. They were confined to the county of Cardigan and a few places in Carmarthenshire, which together were known as the black spot of Wales. To have a son a Unitarian was, therefore, not only a disaster, but a shameful disaster.

All this may seem incredibly light-hearted and irresponsible, but it was not. On the contrary, it was a deadly serious business. It was superficial and shallow—but serious. How could a raw, untutored youth, as I was, possibly decide such great issues as were involved in the controversy between Unitarianism and Trinitarianism? But this is to misconceive the whole process. If one postponed decision or judgment until one had read and studied the evidence for various points of view, one would never be anything at all. Does anybody ever proceed in this fashion? Modern psychology, if it has done nothing else, has completely exposed the fiction that belief and opinion, even in the case of the most exalted intellectualist, are the result of purely ratiocinative processes. Since my conversion to Unitarianism at the age of sixteen was in many ways typical of many later conversions, I describe the process.

After a period of discussion with my Unitarian fellow-student, in which he did most of the talking, I suddenly felt that Unitarianism was the absolute, unchallengeable truth. It could not possibly be anything else. Trinitarian dogmas could be nothing but false. I was amazed that I should ever have believed in them. I then read voraciously everything as a Unitarian, as one already committed. That is to say, I

41

experienced Unitarianism from the inside through being identified with it. It came to mean more to me than a mere creed. It became a totality carrying all my life interests. I came to know Unitarianism not only as a form of belief, for anyone can get to know that without being a Unitarian: I got to know it as a spirit of life, which is only possible from the inside. I came to realize what it meant to *be* Unitarian, what a Unitarian thought, how he felt, how he regarded and reacted to life. I got inside by identification with it.

And that has been the way in which I have since come to know and understand different creeds, philosophies and 'isms. That is how I got to know Marxism many years later. I then thought as a Marxist, felt as a Marxist, from the inside. Though I am no longer Marxist, I nevertheless know how a Marxist *feels*. And that is a priceless possession. One can only get to know a system of thought and life by being the thing itself, by living in the inside of it. In fact, had the thing been possible, I should like to have been a Fascist so as to get to know Fascism on the inside. Unless one gets to know Fascism in that way, there is some element in it which the outsider will miss. But for me, Fascism is for ever impossible. So is Toryism. Yet my experience of Unitarianism, Atheism, Marxism and so on has convinced me that in all the creeds and 'isms with which I disagree, there is some element of passion and pathos, which otherwise a man will miss. The realization of this is corrective of one's pride and egotism.

When, then, I was captured by Unitarianism, I was very fortunate, for my fellow-student took me to see the professor of New Testament Greek at the Presbyterian College. Professor Moore became interested in me and proved himself a very kind mentor. He lent me the very best products of the Unitarian mind, Martineau, Estlin Carpenter, Drummond, L. P. Jacks, Theodore Parker and other American Unitarians. My school studies were woefully neglected, but I believe I was the gainer. At one bound, my intellectual horizon was greatly expanded. I read, with intense absorption, Martineau's *Seat of Authority in Religion*, *A Study of Religion*, and his *Hours of Thought*. The first book was beyond me, but I got a good deal out of the second, which opened my eyes particularly to Church History and to the Philosophy of Religion. Through Estlin Carpenter, my interest was turned to New Testament Criticism: his *First Three Gospels* was an eye-opener, introducing me to a new world. Dr. Drummond further intensified that interest by his studies in the Fourth Gospel. I read the sermons of Parker and Channing and the essays of Emerson, which lifted me upon a new and hitherto unsuspected plane. Professor Moore, who I met once a week, stimulated and encouraged me.

Through this conversion to Unitarianism, I discovered Biblical scholarship, Church history, philosophy, and a wider acquaintance with literature. Through Emerson I came to know Longfellow, Lowell, Whitman and Hawthorne. That led to Carlyle. I read *Heroes* and *The French Revolution*, which excited me in spite of Carlyle's use of the second person and his general apostrophic style, which greatly irritated me. But I was launched on a vast adventure. These were wonderful days, which yielded almost a daily discovery. My inner life, my intellectual development, was so thrilling that the ostracism of my friends at home in chapel hardly troubled me at all.

Some months afterwards I was invited to preach at the Unitarian Church, Aberystwyth. The upshot was that I was asked to become a student minister of the Church. Now I can see the absurdity of it, that a youth of seventeen should minister to a congregation of people. It was of course a very small church, in New Street, behind the University. I preached twice each Sunday. My evening congregation used to number from thirty to forty. I cannot for the life of me imagine how I composed two sermons a week: appalling things they must have been! But the invitation got me out of a difficulty. When I made it clear to my parents that I intended to seek entrance to a Unitarian College, they shut off supplies. Thus, by becoming a student minister, I was enabled to keep myself, and to prepare for the entrance examination to Summerville, the Unitarian College at Victoria Park, Manchester, of which Alexander Gordon was Principal.

I spent about six months in Aberystwyth, during which time I read hard, mainly in philosophy. I shall never forget my first reading of Ferrier's *History of Greek Philosophy*. It made human existence into a problem for me. Then I read Alexander's *Short History of Philosophy*. During that summer I also tackled Plato's *Republic*, Locke and Hume. In fact, those months in Aberystwyth were probably the serenest in my whole life. It was a prolonged period of sustained reading—and thinking. And I was happy, happier probably than I have ever been since. Though life is wonderfully satisfying to me at present, and deeper than it could possibly have been in those far-off summer days by the sea, I was then externally untroubled. I lived in a world of ideas, in which I had a passionate interest for their own sake. Philosophy and literature were my sole reading. I suppose I must have done a certain amount of Latin and Greek and Mathematics; for I got through my entrance examination. So I left Aberystwyth in September for Manchester. I registered at the University as a pre-matriculant, and was supposed to prepare for Matriculation in the following June, but Matriculation vanished, Unitarianism vanished. Manchester was the scene of another revolution in my life.

When I was a student in 1907 Summerville was a residential college. It was very grand to me: a big building in its own grounds. I felt on top of the world, for it was such a contrast to anything I had ever known. I had become one of the privileged sections of the community. It was the only

time I ever did feel that. There were about a dozen or fourteen students in the college. We lived two in a room. I
shared a room with a man of the name of Douglas Hoole,
nearly twice my age. His interests were almost entirely
literary and musical, and I learnt a great deal from him. He
was almost the only student there that took any interest in
me. After the excitement of the first few weeks, I began to
feel a stranger in the place: I simply slept and boarded
there. I attended all my lectures at the University. Once a
week I had to attend a sermon-class, when each student in
turn had to preach a sermon for criticism. That was the only
educational contact I had with the college itself. There was
a very marked and definite prejudice against Welshmen,
which I felt keenly; it conspired to make me feel an alien,
and drove me to find my interests outside. That would
have happened anyhow, but the environment certainly
encouraged that tendency.

At the University I took classes in Latin, Greek, English,
History, Mathematics and Geography. The only teacher
who influenced me was Professor Burrows, and he was the
only one for whom I did any work. He really made Greek
a live subject. We were reading Aeschylus, *Prometheus
Vinctus*. I became fairly proficient in Greek, which was the
only one of the five matriculation subjects I passed. So
interested did I become in Greek literature and history, that
I read Euripides and Sophocles and Aristophanes (in
translation). I also read Grote's *History*. But apart from
Greek, the University course became a dead letter to me.
Hilda Oakeley, who lectured on British History, managed
to divest even that subject of all interest. And our text-
book, Tout's *History of Britain*, was deadly. As time went
on, I used to "cut" as many lectures as I safely could, until
towards the end of the session, like Robert Louis Stephen-
son, I looked in at the University only when I happened to
be passing that way. But that did not mean I was idle. Far
from it. Being an inveterate individualist, I was hunting a

quarry of my own. I was too intellectually awake to be unoccupied.

Early in the session, John Morley, who was Chancellor of the University, visited Manchester to deliver a lecture. He visited the Students' Union and it fell to my lot to hand him a cup of tea. I was immensely thrilled, in spite of the fact that he took not the slightest notice of me. Like his master, John Stuart Mill, he loved humanity in the abstract, but had little eye for the concrete specimen. He had none for me, but that didn't matter. I had handed him a cup of tea! When I excitedly reported this incident to my roommate, Hoole, he was amused and remarked casually: "A great man! Have you read his *Compromise*?" On such insignificant happenings do great things turn.

I read *On Compromise*—and re-read it. Later I devoured the rest of Morley's works, particularly his *Cromwell*, *Rousseau* and *Diderot*. The importance of my discovery lay in two things: first, it bred in me a philosophical interest in politics; and second, it fostered a profound appreciation of individual freedom. Through Morley, I discovered Mill's essay, *On Liberty*, which gave me furiously to think—and his *Political Economy* which started a life-long interest in the subject. The essay on liberty deepened the influence of Morley. I developed a feeling of passionate concern about the liberty of the individual and an intense hatred of tyranny. It led me to many exaggerated expressions and applications of liberty. I have no doubt that I failed to distinguish between licence and liberty, and I realize today that my detestation of tyranny was not quite so pure and objective as I deluded myself into thinking. It camouflaged my native dislike of self-discipline. But when all the debit has been totalled up, the balance, I believe, is still on the credit side. Through Morley and Mill, I enlisted in the ranks of Civilization against Barbarism. It was the radicalism I learnt from Morley and Mill that later enabled me to envisage the peril that was overt in Capitalism, and covert in Socialism, which

Russian Marxism has since made patent with a vengeance. I made another great discovery in Manchester.

One night I was passing the Gaiety Theatre, which was then under the control of Miss Horniman. I had never been in a theatre in my life. In spite of the fact that I had shaken myself free of the Puritan inhibitions of my upbringing, as I thought, I had a strong guilt feeling that evening as I was tempted to go in. It was a *temptation*. And no amount of argument altered the fact that I felt I was doing wrong in entering a theatre—which proves that we should be very careful about what we instil into conscience. I paid my sixpence and the play was Galsworthy's *The Silver Box*. Galsworthy was not even a name to me. But I was fascinated. I shall never forget that night. I hung on every word spoken on the stage. It brought about a revolution in my inner life. I had discovered drama as a vehicle of social discussion.

Thereafter not a week went by without at least one visit to the Gaiety, which proved to be a moral as well as an intellectual school. My first contact with drama was as a serious educational force, not as entertainment. The theatre has never meant anything to me as entertainment merely. During my year at Manchester, I was fortunate beyond words in the opportunities provided by the Gaiety. I saw the plays of Masefield, Galsworthy, Ibsen, Pinero, Henry Arthur Jones and—king of them all—Bernard Shaw. The first play of his I witnessed was *Widowers' Houses*. It made me a white-hot Shaw enthusiast, whom it has taken thirty years to cool down.

What made the Gaiety an experience of still greater significance was that it also opened the door to contemporary writers outside the theatre—chiefly H. G. Wells. It was he who made me a conscious Socialist. I lost both head and heart to Wells. I not only read, I also bought each new book by him, which kept me busy and short of money. He was my guide and philosopher. I raved about him. Yet of all my early gods, he is the one of whom time and experience have made the greatest scarecrow. Today I think Wells merely tawdry, shallow and shabby, with his quack nostrums of World Brain, New Declaration of Human Rights, and so on. But in those Manchester days, my youthful, eager mind clothed him in royal purple. The iconoclasm of his earlier work chimed in perfectly with my own temperamental rebelliousness against authority. Where Wells is concerned I do not want to appear grudging. Though I have long since found him out, I owe him an immense debt of gratitude for sheer intellectual ecstasy and imaginative enjoyment. In those days he was champagne to me.

Wells set the pace for the contemporaries. In his wake came Arnold Bennett and the younger novelists, whom I devoured with great eagerness. But the point I wish to make is that through Wells I acquired a keen interest in contemporary writers which I have never lost. Though my sense of proportion has altered somewhat, and I spend more time with the creative minds of the past, I still am deeply interested in what the new men are saying. That interest I owe to H. G. Wells, for whom I would once have bartered the whole of past literature.

As I say, Wells made me consciously and dominantly a Socialist, and this was another enthusiasm I found in Manchester. On Sunday evenings, the Manchester I.L.P. used to engage a theatre in Peter Street, which was packed to the doors every week by the stars of the party. I heard most of the I.L.P. crusaders, Hardie, Snowden, Ramsay Macdonald, Bruce Glasier, Casey and many others. I would not have missed these meetings for anything, for they came to mean much more to me than Unitarianism, for the ministry of which I was supposed to be training.

Long before the end of the session, in June, 1907, I knew I was never to become a Unitarian minister. That meant I was not to be a minister of any sort. I had come to the point of deep hostility to religion. At first in Manchester, my interests were predominantly religious and philosophical,

48

only to a lesser degree literary; but in a few months I had become a citizen of new worlds—politics, drama, contemporary literature and socialism. In this hothouse of development, my religious life withered away. I became a secularist in the sense of being completely this-worldly, and humanist in the sense of regarding humanity as the only real existence. And I remained secularist and humanist through my later evolution until I found myself at long last in an abyss of despair, in which the fires of suffering burnt all away.

Why then, did I not resign from the college as soon as I realized where I was? For the simple reason that resignation would mean relinquishing the congenial, secure existence of a student, and returning to the coarse struggle and uncertainty of coal-mining. To go back to Maesteg would be purgatory. I shrank from it. It was dishonest and cowardly. Agreed. That was not how I felt about it then, and as I am trying to tell the truth about myself, I cannot pretend. I was not prepared to give up the good food, the superior social status, the marvellous cultural opportunities I was enjoying, to go back to the coal-pit.

This situation typifies the conflict and tension that ruled my life for a long period. I was on the mere edge of security, painfully aware of the brevity of my tenure. It was a disintegrating existence. At the most ecstatic, romantic period of my youth there entered the worm of death.

Things came to a head at the start of the summer term. My terminal results had been so bad that I was ordered to appear before the Principal. Impulsively, I blurted out the truth. He was very human, and advised me to stay on during the summer term, but should I not feel different at the end of it, to send in my resignation. That is what I did. Necessity laid its hand upon me, for during that summer vacation, my father fell ill, and I had to become the breadwinner. My brother was married; my two sisters had become probationer nurses. There was only myself to support an ailing father. I resented it like hell.

D
49

4

So, back to the pit! That was crash number one in my life! It made me bitter and resentful. I blamed society, not myself. I wallowed in self-pity. How dreadful that I, David Richard Davies, a cultured, brilliant, sensitive youth, should be forced to consort with the foul-mouthed, coarse, ignorant clodhoppers who were my work-mates! That is what I felt. In retrospect I see the funny side of it. But it wasn't funny at the time—far from it.

It is important to note that education had made no fundamental moral difference to me, except to intensify my egotism and inflate my pride. Its net effect was to isolate me from my fellows. My increased knowledge, wider interests, deeper culture resulted in my becoming a greater, more miserable sinner. When I left Manchester to resume work in the coal-mine, I was certainly a better educated man than when I left the pit to go to school. Morally I was no better. Indeed, I was worse. My egocentricity had certainly grown deeper, for I now disliked and despised the people among whom necessity had replaced me. A better education had made me less sociable. It has been a long-cherished assumption that education automatically makes men morally better. This assumption experience negates, as it certainly did in me.

Though in my first real big battle with life, I had been worsted, it did not teach me humility: it fortified my pride. I had to undergo incredible suffering and descend the depths of despair before I realized wherein my true peace lay. Meanwhile, what I saw in my failure was the conspiracy of an unjust society. It was at this point that the earlier experience of poverty became fully conscious in me. I cursed society. And now that I had become definitely socialist, society meant the capitalist system. It was the system that was evil. *I* was innocent. In my individual life, I was experiencing the frustration and self-delusion of an era. I was recapitulating in myself the disaster of our modern world. My experience was that of the world in microcosm.

From July, 1907, to September, 1912, a period of five years, I worked as a miner, except for a brief interlude of a few months, when I went to sea, which I shall narrate in the proper place. In due course I got over the pangs and bitterness of leaving college and became absorbed in my activities. Romantic youth, after all, has a resilience of its own, and, as yet, experience had not sufficiently tamed or de-vitalized it. It is very, very rarely that life can give to vigorous youth a knock-out blow. The humiliation of having to return to manual labour stunned me only temporarily. My native vitality returned and I was soon in the thick of trade-union activity, I.L.P. propaganda, Women's Suffrage agitation, and, at last, even preaching once again. In that Indian summer of my pre-war capitalist world, youth had a wonderful time.

At first I remained outside the Church altogether. When I had gone over to Unitarianism, my membership in the Congregational Church at home lapsed and I did not resume it for some time, which was a source of grief to my mother and of conflict with my father. On Sundays, I stayed at home, or went for long tramps up the mountain. They were difficult days. They gave me a suppressed guilt-feeling.

I soon became active in the Miners' Federation. Early in 1908, I was elected a member of the Library Committee. In Maesteg, the miners had several Miners' Institutes under their control, to which they contributed at the rate of one penny per pound of wages earned. In these Institutes, there were billiard rooms, reading rooms and a lending library administered by the miners themselves. I became an Institute committee-man, and my main interest was, of course, the library. Through my friendship with the librarian, Harry Lee, most of my recommendations for new books were accepted. I was thus in the fortunate position of being able to read new books soon after their publication. In the ordinary course of events, on a wage of only a few pounds a week, new books would have been out of the question, but as a member of a Library Committee, they became available for me before they went on the shelves. Thus I did not suffer, in this respect, as compared with my student days.

I read voraciously, never with greater zest than during these hectic years. My main subject was Economics. I became familiar with Marx—without understanding him—that came later. Adam Smith, Ricardo, Mill, Cairnes and Marshall I came to know fairly thoroughly. Before I was twenty I had gained a fair grasp of economic theory and economic and trade-union history. I also steeped myself in Fabian essays and pamphlets. But I also read much in literature, especially the later Victorians. Hardy and Meredith were the great discoveries of this period—Hardy particularly. There must be some deep strain of pessimism in me; for his writings always appealed strongly to me. Kipling and Dickens I also read. Scott I did not care for. Thackeray I detested: I tried *Vanity Fair* and gave it up. In addition, I read a good deal of the R.P.A. sixpennies. They were great value. The polemics of Joseph McCabe I especially enjoyed.

I believe it was in 1909 that I became a member of the Lodge Executive. Each pit constituted a "lodge", that is, a branch of the Federation. Its affairs were administered by an elected executive, of which I became a member. So I became familiar with the day-to-day work of my union. This consisted of such matters as fighting pit disputes with the management, of which there was an abundance; administering the newly-passed Workmen's Compensation Act; combating non-unionism, etc. Frequently I acted as a delegate to District and South Wales Conferences held at Cardiff. They were memorable days, which brought me into contact with many men who were later destined to play an important part in national affairs, notably Frank Hodges and A. J. Cook. I was in the van of the new Industrial Unionism movement, which began to agitate the South Wales coalfield at that time. The four or five years preceding the outbreak of the Great War in 1914 were a very stormy period in South Wales. They witnessed a succession of great strikes. No miner could deny the existence of a class-struggle, because he suffered it daily in his own flesh and blood. It was about that time, too, that there was published a pamphlet called *The Miner's Next Step*, which caused a great stir. It advocated industrial action for paralysing coal-production under capitalist ownership, with the object of expropriating the owners. It was an attempt to apply in South Wales the Syndicalism which Sorel and others were preaching in France. With that movement I became closely associated.

It was about this time, too, that Vernon Hartshorn was appointed Miners' Agent for the Maesteg district, so that I came to know him well. With him and a few others, I was responsible for establishing a Sunday Evening Forum in Maesteg, which ran for many years. We had well-known speakers every week to address us on topics of the day. At that time the coal valleys were intellectually and politically alive.

Alongside these trade-union activities went keen political work as well. I became a member of the I.L.P., which in those days was a strong and influential party, and under the chairmanship of Keir Hardie, partook somewhat of the character of a religious crusade. It satisfied my religious yearnings, for socialism became a religion in which I developed an unquestioned, dogmatic faith. Its future triumph I never doubted. It would solve all problems and put everything right. I looked upon the party leaders as heroes and prophets.

It was under the auspices of the I.L.P. that I learnt the art of public speaking, in which I flatter myself I found at least one thing I could do supremely well: for I could hold an audience. It was on I.L.P. soap-boxes that I served my apprenticeship, night after night, up and down the valleys, addressing open-air meetings, until I became self-confident and proficient. Open-air meetings and the heckler have never had any terrors for me, for I graduated in too hard a school. Years later I addressed open-air meetings in Hyde Park, the grave of the weak and incompetent, but I survived, even flourished, for after my early training in I.L.P. propaganda in Wales it was easy going.

I met with a good deal of hostility—a surprising fact, but true. But the opposition I had to contend with in the valleys as a socialist was pale compared with what I had to meet as an advocate of Women's Suffrage. Many a night did I tramp over the mountains to address angry audiences on the subject of votes for women. It was my only activity which succeeded in making my mother angry. It made her "feel ashamed" of me. Votes for women indeed! Much better for them to stay at home and read their Bible!

5

In the midst of all this, I began to develop serious eye-trouble, nystagmus. I went to the Swansea Hospital and was told that, if I wanted to save my eyesight, I should have to give up coal-mining. That was a bombshell! My father was laid aside by a serious illness. I was the only breadwinner. What was to be done?

I secured a job on the pit surface at the same colliery. That became a nightmare, and is still a nightmare as I look back over the years. It was not the work itself, but the foreman who was in charge. The work was certainly not pleasant, it consisted of loading heavy timber in all weathers. It was hard and exhausting, but the foreman made it hell.

I have been in all sorts of rough circumstances. I have worked in the stokehold of a tramp steamer and roughed it in doss-houses. But never have I met so coarse, cruel, sadistic a monster as that foreman. And to make matters worse, he was a deacon in one of the Welsh Independent chapels.

For a long time he made me very bitter towards the Church. A huge, ugly, mis-shapen man, with rolls of fat all over him, for ever bullying, shouting, and bumping the men about, an almost exact prototype of the Nazi concentration camp guard. He made my days an utter misery. But I was in a trap of circumstance. An ailing father at home alone made me endure it. I determined that the very first day he started work, I should abandon the job.

One day, when about half a dozen of us were loading 15 ft. timber on to a truck in driving wind and sleet, the foreman's bullying became unendurable; he seemed to concentrate his venom on me. At last, he got hold of me by the scruff of the neck as I had my arms under a heavy piece of timber, and pushed me. Something snapped inside me. I dropped my arms, picked up a bar of iron and in cold fury would have killed him, but for the intervention of my fellow labourers. I told him that one day I would "do" for him. After that episode he left me severely alone. The manager tried to get rid of me, but the union made that impossible, for my dismissal would have stopped the colliery.

But the day of my release arrived. My father, after an illness of years, started work again. And I stopped. On the day I finished, I waited to waylay the foreman on his way home from the colliery and I set about that corpulent mass good and hard. With foot and fist I knocked the stuffing out of him. I suppose he was about sixty years of age. What did I care! Like all bullies, he was a craven coward, and his squeals and grunts made it all the sweeter. It took him a long time to return to shatter the air at Siloh chapel with his stentorian prayers. To kick and punch him, as I did, was not Christian, but it was very human. I'm no saint! It was a sheer ecstasy.

The day after my father resumed work I left home. I went to Swansea, and for six or seven months my parents saw nothing of me: I did not even write to them. It was cruel and I am certainly repentant for such neglect. But I was bitter. At Swansea, I signed on as a stoker on a merchant tramp steamer and the same night sailed for New York. To stoke a tramp across the Atlantic in 1910 was hell—a big hell. The terrible food, the close quarters, the unbelievable coarseness of the men, and the exhausting labour! But I survived, for one could not sit in a corner and die. From New York I returned to Liverpool, louse-eaten and wretched. There are certainly better ways of seeing the world than from a stoker's port-hole.

From Liverpool I crossed the ferry to Birkenhead and got into the Church Army home, where I was de-loused, for which I am eternally grateful to Carlile and his devoted assistants. They provided me with new underwear. But I fear I have to record an ungrateful immediate response, for after one night I just walked off. Then for several months I tramped the English countryside, doing odd jobs, sleeping in work-houses, picking oakum, helping myself in the orchards of Herefordshire, and for a week I fed a couple of lions and tigers in a travelling menagerie.

One day I suddenly realized what a fool I was. To tramp about, to live from hand to mouth, no home, no books. Something broke inside me, and under the late summer stars I determined to make for home. I wrote the first letter to my mother since I had left home six months or so ago. The letter was unstamped. I asked her to post five shillings to me addressed to the General Post Office, Cardiff. I arrived at Cardiff early on Saturday, and found the letter awaiting me, with a postal order. I bought a pipe, a box of matches, an ounce of tobacco, and at a dockside restaurant, a gargantuan meal. Improvident to the last, I had not left myself enough to pay my fare home. But I set off gaily to walk the nineteen miles to Bridgend. I arrived in time for the last train to Maesteg, having enough for the ticket with a penny or two to spare. I reached home after midnight; the prodigal had returned. Though my ailing father had gone to bed, mother was waiting. God bless her wonderful soul!

She had a hot bath ready, and a supper of my favourite dish, tea, bread and butter and kidney beans. Then she talked to me. That was typical: she saw to my physical needs first, then addressed herself to my soul. I shall never forget her words: "Don't you see, my boy, that the way of the sinner is hard?" So gentle, so uncomplaining, so full of mercy and compassion. She uttered not a single word of blame. She was overjoyed to have me home again, safe and sound. From the day I had left, she had kept the door unlocked. Wonderful mother!

I experienced that night some kind of conversion. I can say no more than that. I got a glimpse of myself—and was not flattered.

Despite my treatment of the foreman I got employment underground at the same colliery. I went back to chapel, and the urge to renew my preparation for the ministry became strong. When I definitely decided upon this and had been accepted as a candidate by Bradford United College, I asked the colliery manager to give me a job as a night-labourer, which he did. I started work at 9.30 p.m. and finished at 5.30 a.m. I was in bed by 7 a.m. and slept until midday. Then I read and studied between seven and eight hours a day in preparation for the entrance to Bradford. I got a little private coaching in mathematics, always my bugbear. But I trained myself, from the text-books, in Latin, Greek, English, history and scripture. I wrote out lists of Greek and Latin verbs, together with their principal parts, and took them with me to my work for memorization. I had a most generous work-mate, who used to do a goodly share of my work so that I might learn my verbs. He was fascinated with the Greek characters I used to chalk on the coal-face, which made a splendid blackboard. It was very strenuous, but immensely exhilarating.

So at the end of June, 1912—or was it 1913—I sat my entrance to United College. I felt myself to be a veteran among the schoolboys who sat with me. There I met Dr.

Griffith-Jones for the first time. He took a warm interest in me and put me at my ease. I was informed that I had satisfied the examiners and been accepted, so I made a bee-line for the post office to wire the good news home.

On that brilliant June night, as I sat in Manningham Park, listening to a military band, the world seemed very wonderful, serene, secure. I was happy. Had I not struggled through the defeats and vicissitudes of five long years to triumph, to achievement? Once again the world was good, and I was a rather remarkable fellow. Miner, trade-union official, political agitator, marine-stoker, tramp, embryonic lion-tamer—and now a student once again! Rather wonderful, I thought! What was uppermost in my mind was not the goodness of God, but consciousness of my own quality. D.R. occupied the centre of the stage. In Manningham Park in 1912 there was no hint of disaster. My generation and I were perfectly at one. Its security and golden promise were to crash in the world war only two years distant. And my hard-won triumph was but overture to my own greater disaster and despair.

CHAPTER IV

UNIVERSITY AND COLLEGE

OCTOBER, 1912, found me at United College, Bradford, preparing for the Edinburgh University Preliminary Examination, which is the Scottish equivalent of matriculation. Yorkshire United College sent its students to Edinburgh for their Arts course, and gave a preliminary Arts year under the tuition of Dr. Ambrose Pope. I was one of a class of five or six. During that first session, I kept my nose to the grindstone and worked hard. At the age of twenty-three I was doing what amounted to schoolboy's work, and competing with youths from secondary and public schools. Yet I had to get through the Scottish Universities Preliminary to get a chance to graduate. I confined myself more rigorously to the subjects of the curriculum during this Arts year in Bradford than I had ever done before—or have done since.

There was very little of note in my first session. Dr. Pope was not inspiring. He was great on system and was certainly efficient, so that he pulled me through the Preliminary without much difficulty—Latin, Greek, English, history and mathematics. Mathematics at Edinburgh was absurdly easy—even so, it is a mystery how I got through. The day before my departure for Edinburgh, Dr. Pope invited me to have tea with him, when he pressed me to act on a suggestion which he had always found effective. He advised me to spend five minutes—not a few, but exactly five—reading my examination questions over slowly and carefully. "By the time you have done that, Mr. Davies, there is sure to be *one* question which you will be able to answer easily. Do that first, and you will then have confidence to answer the next question." He made it sound so easy that

I acted on his advice, but it did not work. After staring at the mathematics paper for five minutes, I picked out my easy question, a simple vulgar fraction. But something went wrong, for I covered sheet after sheet with figures, and spent an hour on that easy question, getting nowhere. I cursed Dr. Pope and his system, and with sinking heart tackled what I could of the rest of the paper. I got through, more by the kind-heartedness of the examiner, I am sure, than by any evidence of my own knowledge.

During the first year at Bradford, I did a considerable amount of preaching. It was the custom for the churches to request the services of students for pulpit duty on Sundays, so that I preached in the country round about Bradford and sometimes much further afield, once travelling as far as Sunderland, where I first saw an aeroplane in flight.

My Edinburgh University career was cut short by a nervous breakdown, but I had enjoyed Lodge's lectures on European History, Mair's on Greek, and Pringle-Pattison's (S.P.[2] as he used to be known) on logic and metaphysics. I got into Professor Nicholson's bad books by challenging his theories on political economy. He was a crusted Conservative, and in an essay I flatly contradicted his entire teaching and championed Marx's theory of surplus value, of which I had only an imperfect grasp. But I had had too much experience of working-class struggles to be taken in by the pedantic apologetics the Professor ground out in lecture after lecture. He took it very badly, and made it clear that I was there to learn *his* theories, not to air my own. After that I never took him seriously, and during his lectures I went day-dreaming.

But I was drained of vitality. For two years I had been at it without cessation. A year before entering college I had been working night and day, and was equally busy throughout my first year in college. During vacations, I was back working at the colliery, which lack of finance made necessary. Although I was awarded a Brown scholarship of £60 per annum, and in addition a grant of £20, it cost more than £80 a year. So I had to utilize my vacations to earn money, which I did in the colliery and by preaching. Under the strain I gave way.

Then, after consultation with Dr. E. Griffith-Jones, it was decided that I should not return to Edinburgh, but proceed to Bradford for the theological course. I was already twenty-five or six years of age. I should be getting on for thirty, at the earliest, before getting to the ministry—which was late. So I had to bid a reluctant farewell to Edinburgh.

During the summer vacation before entering on theology, I became student-pastor at the Horton Bank Top Congregational Church, just outside Bradford. It was understood I was to take matters easy and get myself fit for the winter's work, which is what I did. I preached and did little else.

I

Meanwhile, the World War had come! It reduced my theological course almost to nothing. The hectic patriotism of Dr. Griffith-Jones threw an air of futility and insignificance over the college. So obsessed was he by the war that the theological education of the students became a matter of secondary importance. He spent most of his time recruiting for the army or on propaganda missions in the United States.

Of Hebrew, Old Testament Theology, Religion, History and Criticism I learnt practically nothing. The professor, Dr. Archibald Duff, was a most unfortunate man for the job, and he found me impossible. I was probably his worst student. At the entrance Hebrew examination, he awarded me the record of exactly o marks. For that performance, I got into trouble with the Education Committee, who deprived me of £10 of my grant and warned me that I should have to secure 60 per cent. of marks at the next examination under threat of dismissal. I must have gained the marks; for

not only was I not dismissed, I was granted my leaving certificate in due course. But of Dr. Duff's lectures I took not
the slightest notice. He became zealously patriotic and his
lectures frequently ended in anti-German tirades. I was
equally strongly pacifist, and the effect of using the Old
Testament as a course for patriotic propaganda was infuri-
ating to me. The effect was that only after I settled in the
ministry did I really begin to study the Old Testament.

Though Duff was a poor teacher, he was very kindly,
friendly and approachable. He was always a great talker but
never listened. Even when he stopped speaking, he did not
listen. One could see him getting ready for the next spurt.
In the end, I did not attempt to discuss anything with him,
but he was a man for whom I had, and still have, an affectionate regard.

From two other professors, Dr. Alexander Grieve, afterwards Principal of Lancashire College, and Professor Price,
who became Principal of United College, I learnt much in
different ways. Dr. Grieve gave his students the impression
of competence, of really knowing his subject—and no
nonsense. And he made one work. He was not an inspiration, never indulged in flights of imagination, his feet were
always on solid earth; but he had the knack of communi-
cating information, and by his very air made one feel the
tremendous importance of his subject. And so I paid real
attention to New Testament study, which I developed after
I left college. He was a real friend, with a great human heart,
who regarded his students as human beings. He was the
only one of the staff who enquired about your parents. He
was a man of intuition, too. He used to tell me that my
career would be stormy, "But you'll come through"! he
assured me. I never forget his prayer at my Ordination
Service in 1919.

From Professor Price I learned the meaning and value of
historic method in the study of Church History and the
History of Christian Doctrine. His first lecture on the Medi-

terranean environment of early Christianity is still vivid in my mind; it excited me and accentuated what was already strong, a deep interest in history. His lectures were all too few. In January, 1916, the Governors decided to close the college, and arranged for those students who did not join the armed forces to read under the guidance of the professors. But the decision became a dead letter. Early in January, 1916, I returned as student pastor of the little Congregational Church at Horton Bank Top, which had a long tradition of student-ministers. I took my place in that apostolical succession of United students and was there from January to the following September, living an acutely divided life. My life was not co-ordinated, but proceeded in self-contained exclusive spheres; pacifist interests, work in the church, and theological reading, with the war overshadowing everything. My pacifist activities outside the church were a cause of offence to those who were incensed that a healthy young fellow like myself was allowed to escape war duty, when so many of their own sons had to join the army. The path of a pacifist minister in war-time is bound to be thorny, be he ever so discreet, and I was anything but discreet. Now and again, I came out with uncompromising pacifist utterances which outraged many people. The member who was the financial mainstay of the church finally stated that he would not attend the church so long as I remained. For the first time I tasted in my own flesh one of the grave defects of the Free Church ministry, that the minister is dependent for his bread and butter on the people to whom he preaches. After eight months, in September I resigned.

2

The first world war and my reaction to it were the outstanding events of my theological course at Bradford. Theological study and even preaching took second place.

I was a fanatical pacifist—really aggressive and offensive. At this distance of time I despair of the attempt to describe the processes by which I became pacifist. I fancy that I was actuated mainly by acute political opposition, which—all unconsciously—I disguised in a religious form. Brailsford's *War of Steel and Gold* (one of the finest studies of modern imperialism) was much more active in my mind than the New Testament. In form my pacifism was religious, in content it was political.

Deep down, I have little doubt that my pacifism was to some degree a rationalization of physical cowardice, for I recall elaborate, strenuous attempts to make it clear that cowardice had nothing to do with it. I comforted myself with the assurance that I was exhibiting courage of a higher order in resisting the social will to war. Since those days I have had a little experience of modern war, and I know that fear is a very real thing, though less fearful in the event than in the anticipation. Fear animates all men, including conscientious objectors. Pacifism enabled me to avoid the thing I feared, and for that reason probably came easily to me. No idealism or philosophy—or theology—can possibly be one hundred per cent. objective. Man's original sin penetrates even his loftiest aspirations and purest achievements.

But though fear was one of the unconscious roots of my pacifism, it was by no means the only one. I was acutely aware of the anti-Christian character of war, and could not reconcile war with Christianity. I thought it best not to try, for the attempt to do so led to appalling confusion and hypocrisy. Since war and Christianity are irreconcilable, I concluded, no Christian could take part in it.

Let the reader bear in mind that I was an out-and-out Modernist; that, in particular, I believed the Kingdom of God to be something which Man could himself achieve. Given that assumption, there is something to be said for pacifism. But that belief begs the whole question. The Kingdom of God is the gift of God; it is utterly beyond human capacity to create that kingdom on earth or heaven. War is simply the *final* manifestation of self-will, that is, of Man's radical sin. How can I entertain a conscientious objection to its final manifestation without having an equally conscientious objection to all other manifestations? Which reduces the question to absurdity. I never thought of that. Original sin was a theological barbarism I had long since transcended; I fanatically pursued the delusion that by being pacifist I was building the Kingdom.

At least I practised what I preached. I participated in strenuous pacifist propaganda outside the Church and preached it inside the church. I joined the Fellowship of Reconciliation, and was one of the original foundation, along with Henry Hodgkin, Hugh Martin, the Rev. Leyton Richards, and Dr. Richard Roberts and others. The Bradford Branch met every week at the Friends' Meeting House, and though I attended the meetings regularly and did a good deal of propaganda in the Bradford Area, my zeal was mainly expressed through the No-Conscription Fellowship, which was a very live affair. Through it I got to know and to work with many local and national political figures.

During those war years, I became acquainted with Ramsay Macdonald and addressed an anti-war meeting with him at Leeds, afterwards travelling with him to South Wales; later I met him in Bradford, at the house of William Leach, M.P., who dispensed a generous political hospitality. I am certain that the Ramsay Macdonald of later years, the darling of the duchesses, was a far different man from the ostracized figure of those stressful years. Many harsh judgments have been passed on him, but I found him a companionable, likeable man, with something very wistful about him. He talked very freely, especially about his theological reading and beliefs. How my interest was kindled when he told me he had been friends with Dr. Fairbairn! One thing he said about Fairbairn stuck in my mind, that when he entered the ministry he was at his desk every morning, winter and summer alike at 6 a.m., which I thought to be wonderful. I referred to Macdonald's little biography of his wife and he spoke quite freely about her, and there can be no doubt about the great regard in which he held her, or about the great influence she had exercised upon him. Had she lived, European history might have taken a different turn, and she might have neutralized some of the poison of power in the first Labour Prime Minister.

Another interesting figure was Charles Trevelyan, M.P., as he then was. But the most vivid of my friends was Dr. Orchard, a friendship that lasted until he went over to Rome. During those war years I saw a good deal of him, and afterwards for many years we met at regular intervals. He was a dynamo of a man, and fond of good stories about himself. As, for instance, when Dr. Forsyth, Principal of Hackney College, was once asked what he thought of him —"Orchard?" he sniffed, "Froth! But champagne froth!" Another was of a visit to Westminster Chapel, on the Sunday when Dr. J. H. Jowett started his ministry there on his return from New York; it so happened that Orchard had a free Sunday, so he and his wife went to hear Jowett. They arrived a good hour before the service began, to find the place already full. Turning towards his wife, Orchard whispered: "Do you see, my dear, I could never fill a church like this." And she replied: "No, but you could *empty* it." As they used to say in Bradford, she had him taped.

These experiences in Bradford yielded most valuable knowledge of men and affairs, but played havoc with theological study. Yet they stimulated reading in other directions, chiefly economic and political. But I lived, if cheaply. Once again, the problem of making ends meet became acute. With the closing of the college, grants ceased, and when I resigned my student-pastorate the shillings became few. I managed to rent a tiny cottage a few miles outside Bradford at three-and-six a week, and lived the so-called "simple" life.

It was anything but simple. I had to walk more than a mile to fetch water. By the time I prepared my meals and cleaned and tidied up, there was left little time—and less inclination —for reading and study. Fortunately, it did not last long.

In the summer of 1917 I preached one Sunday at Ravensthorpe Congregational Church. The pastorate was vacant. I must have made an impression, for I was asked, discreetly, if I were in a position to accept a call. After a few months of negotiation with the church and college authorities, it was decided that I could go to Ravensthorpe as a student-minister on the understanding that I should be ordained when the war was over, by which time I should have gained my leaving certificate. And so it fell out. I entered upon my ministry there in September, 1917, and was ordained in October, 1919, remaining there until October, 1922, five years of storm with fitful intervals of sunshine.

CHAPTER V

EARLY DAYS IN THE MINISTRY

I STARTED UPON my ministry with a varied assortment of goods in my bag, but amongst them the one essential, fundamental thing was lacking—an experimental knowledge of God as Judge and Redeemer. I had a keen and passionate interest in political and social problems, and a fair knowledge of them—certainly I knew more about these things than the average minister, which is not saying much. I was widely though not deeply read in literature and philosophy. Of history I knew a great deal. I had but little more than an elementary smattering of theology in its various branches, and certainly no scholarship.

I was possessed of an imperturbable optimism, which I set down here to my amazement, symptomatic, not only of my own personal blindness, but as a child of my time. Though it was in the midst of a world war, my confidence in human power to fashion Utopia was untouched. My gospel was a human gospel. The "good news" heralded by Christ was the native goodness and potentiality of man; this had been overlaid by the morbid deviations of theological orthodoxy, and by an anti-Christian capitalism; the classic concentration upon sin had obscured the original, sunny simple gospel of Jesus. I had fallen victim to the whole Modernist development, especially the German contribution. My one disagreement with the German theologians was the stiff prices at which their books were published. I paid twenty-five shillings for Harnack's *Mission and Expansion of Christianity in the First Three Centuries* (a book I greatly valued and still value), and three pounds ten shillings for his *History of Dogma*.

The core of the preaching was the unquestioned capacity

of man to build the Kingdom of God upon earth. This was to be done by social action, by embodying what I thought of as the principle of love in the structure of the State, and social institutions. More and more I came to think of Jesus as a social revolutionary with a programme of political action, the objective of which was to establish on earth a perfect civilization. Therefore, my first task, as I conceived it, was to inoculate my congregation with a set of ideas, and for five years I hopefully persisted in my offensive on those tough Yorkshire brains.

I should be painting an absurdly false picture if I implied that my preaching was consciously, systematically, planned Sunday by Sunday with such an end in view. What happened week by week was haphazard, spontaneous and impulsive. I was faced with the necessity of having to turn out every week two sermons, a week-night address and a children's address—the latter the bane of my life. I confess that, more often than not, I appropriated ready-made addresses from printed volumes of children's talks. Publishers of such books are great benefactors to many ministers, whatever they may be to the children. But I never once used another man's sermon. Of course, I have often made use of leading ideas from sermons, but I always treated them in my own way. But that practice was confined to the first years in my ministry. I contemplated with shrinking heart the task of producing three addresses a week. Often and often, I was in a panic on a Friday or Saturday, when I had no idea what I should preach. But something always came. I seldom found the standard remedies of much help to me. For instance, the veterans advised young ministers to keep a notebook handy, and to jot down a text that struck their imagination, together with notes of leading ideas. I followed that advice, but it never worked. In my hour of need, those notes refused to catch fire. What I did was to "skim" the Bible, read page after page rapidly, until a text struck my eye. Many a sermon which originated in that fashion "went well". Sterility of imagination is sometimes a blessing in disguise.

But I did preach what I believed. I did not hide my light under a bushel. There was hardly a sermon in those last two war years into which I did not, somehow or other, bring in my anti-war dogma, and I often devoted whole sermons to it. I must have felt myself very deeply driven to do this, because I shrank from the rows that so frequently followed. Contrary to the impression many people have of me, I hate to be at variance with my fellow-men. In a public career of forty years, the unpopular causes I have espoused have earned me enmity and bitterness, which have caused me deep misery and unhappiness. My pacifist preaching in my first church was no exception. In my entire congregation, only two persons were pacifist. The rest were a solid hostile phalanx. Why, therefore, did I persist?

One reason, I am still convinced, was my personal conviction that it was the right thing to do, that I was driven to it. Was this something prophetic? Dr. Kraemer has defined a prophet as "a man who is driven by a force greater than himself". In a deep, obscure way, I did feel driven. I walked with a soft tread, whenever I could, and was always happy on the rare occasions when the preferences of my congregation coincided with my own inclinations. Deliberately to have invited hostility, when I so much quailed under it is evidence, I think, that a prophetic urge drove me on.

Yet I am under no illusion that that was the whole story —far from it. Modern psychology, especially the work of Freud and Adler, has demonstrated beyond reasonable doubt the all-pervading influence of unconscious egotism. Which is only another way of saying what the Bible says, that man is born into a kingdom of sin. The "inferiority-feeling" (Adler) with which every son of Adam is born drives man to some form or other of compensation. My inclination for unpopular preaching was therefore, in part, due to my desperate need to convince myself that I was somebody, that

I could not be ignored. Obviously, preaching provocative pacifism in the midst of a great war did make me a public figure. I became the centre of a maelstrom. Whilst it gave me acute misery, I yet derived an exquisite satisfaction from it. I got the feeling that I was somebody to be reckoned with. This illustrates, of course, the inevitable tension of thought and behaviour to which men are subject. If all men are liars, all are also self-contradictory. So, believing that I was the pure servant of truth, in fact I was utilizing the truth as a mode of personal exhibitionism. Vanity? But then vanity is a peculiar disease of preachers, especially of the star variety. Not, of course, that I was a star preacher. Though I honestly confess that, at one time, the desire to become one was a constant theme of my day-dreaming.

Social problems constituted my other leading subject. Here again, I sailed very near the wind. Before long I was being accused of preaching Socialism. It was quite true. I could see hardly anything else in the Bible at that time, especially in the prophets. I preached on all sorts of social topics—the necessity for a good peace, the need for industrial reorganization, the reshaping of education, and the development of social services. I was comprehensive. I definitely affirmed the anti-Christian character of Capitalism, and the necessity for Socialism. This caused nasty differences between myself and the business men in the Church, in particular with a prominent Liberal politician, a man of great ability and, personally, very likeable. The acrimony between us was tempered by a certain amount of good will.

So much of my own life and thought was absorbed in social activity that very little energy went into purely personal things. Consequently my preaching lacked the personal note. I hardly thought of my congregation as individuals, preoccupied by their own needs and troubles. My one aim was to get society right. If we could abolish war and poverty, I thought, people would automatically become happy and virtuous. I realize only too well how "the hungry sheep looked up and were not fed". I gave them ideas, but no Gospel. How could I give Good News when I myself had no living experience of Redemption?

I

But preaching was only one activity of my ministry, though by far the most important. The other was pastoral visitation, so-called. As far as my experience goes, the kind of visitation of people usually practised by the Free Church ministry is more social than pastoral. I do not presume for a moment to pass judgment on it, but to me it was distasteful and wearying, as an appalling waste of time. I always resented the hours I spent talking trifles with people, when I could have been using it in my study. I am simply recording this as a fact.

I began with good intentions. I determined to visit all the members of my church and congregation systematically, so as to get to know them all in their own homes. And with the idea of getting the men-folk, I did my visiting at night after they had returned from work. This memory is still a nightmare. The housing conditions were such that serious talk of any kind was practically impossible. All the family were gathered in the one room, all bent on their pursuits. One could talk only of inconsequential things—the weather, local gossip, the external aspect of church events, and similar things. I gained no personal contact from such meetings. After two or three hours a night of such visiting, I became deeply angry and frustrated.

Among the well-to-do minority of the church, living conditions of course were different, but my experience became no more encouraging. At my first visit to a textile manufacturer who seldom came to church, things went wrong from the start. Conversation inevitably veered to the war, and my pacifist opinions aroused deep resentment. The visit ended in a storm, when the good man, with Yorkshire bluntness, told me he did not want to see me again—a sentiment that I reciprocated on the spot, most heartily. That example, however, was the worst. I became friendly, in a superficial sort of way, with three other well-to-do families, with one of whom I had some intellectual and spiritual fellowship. This, however, did not survive the discovery that I was a very imperfect human being.

I soon abandoned any pretence at such pastoral visitation. The only visits I made thereafter were to my sick members and these, to the best of my ability, I performed faithfully. They had little value, however, because I was fundamentally isolated from the people. Here again, the beginnings proved unfortunate. I visited an old lady who had been ill for some time. After talking a little while about her complaints and their medical treatment, I suddenly asked her if she would like me to offer prayer. She replied "tha' can please thyssen". That answer, apparently such a little thing, gave me an anti-prayer complex. After that, in sick visiting I found praying an extraordinarily difficult thing and very rarely offered it. In fact, I had to feel very intimate with people before I could bring myself to pray with them. Nearly all my sick visiting was done only from a sense of duty, and therefore had little value. I got no satisfaction from it. Performance of duty, done merely as duty or out of a sense of compulsion, is arid. Unless it is absorbed by love, it has no living quality.

Inevitably, I was inwardly isolated from my people, and except for one or two, drifted away from them all. I lived in a world of my own—an abstract, intellectual world. My gospel was nothing but a system of ideas to which the rank-and-file of my church did not respond. Beyond these ideas, I had nothing to say. I became more and more a misfit. What was once said of a celebrated Anglican could probably have been said of me, that during the week I was invisible and on Sundays I was incomprehensible. It is with sadness that I recall those first years in the ministry.

2

Partly as a result of this situation I sought satisfaction in activities outside the ministry. Through my friendship with Oswald Jones, then editor of the *Dewsbury Reporter*, I became interested in the work of the Poetry Society, helped to found a branch in Dewsbury, and was appointed its first chairman. In that uncompromising centre of the "rag trade", about fifty to sixty people got together week after week for the study of English poetry, past and present, when a paper was read, or readings given, sometimes by contemporary poets. I looked forward to these meetings with much greater zest than to the weekly devotional meetings in my own church.

The Poetry Society brought me into touch with people altogether outside the Church—for whom, indeed, the Church did not exist. All unconsciously, I moved a step further towards the conclusion that the Church was not indispensable. Here I found people who were intensely more intellectually alive and alert than any church people I knew. The contrast did not increase my zeal for ministerial work. I began to breathe the atmosphere in which Biblical Christianity was irrelevant. Curiously enough, this fortified me in my Modernism, in the belief that to appeal to the world of today the Church would have to undergo a drastic theological overturn. What I failed to realize was that religion of any sort had become irrelevant to the modern mind. Without knowing it, I had begun to develop in myself the mentality to which Christianity would no longer be necessary. This process was to take another seven or eight years before coming to full fruition.

Through my work for the Poetry Society, I was invited to conduct classes in English Literature at the Dewsbury Technical Institute, which I did for two winter sessions. It was work I much enjoyed. In the first session I lectured on Greek drama, using Dr. Gilbert Murray's incomparable translations. I do not know what benefit, if any, my pupils derived, but I profited greatly. For to teach is one very good way of learning. During that winter I read assiduously the plays of Euripides, Sophocles and Aeschylus. With *The Trojan Women*, and its tremendous indictment of war, the class was turned into an anti-war debating society. I am afraid it was not a good preparation for examinations, but my students caught something of the wonderful spirit of Greek drama.

Another activity was with the Save-the-Children Fund. I toured the district addressing public meetings and church gatherings, and I like to think that, as a result of what I did in co-operation with others, many children were kept alive in the Vienna of the post-war years. In moments of fantasy I picture many of those children, now grown to manhood and womanhood. But who knows? Such is the tragic contradiction of our human lot, that perhaps many lived only to become the brutal destroyers of European civilization.

My one direct incursion into politics during this period was to support Sir John Simon at the Spen-Valley by-election in 1919. For the first and only time I deserted the Labour and Socialist cause. The country was then being governed by the Lloyd-George Coalition, and (as I believed) governed badly. My opposition to that Government was so great as to amount to hatred: at all costs, I reasoned, the most important thing was to secure the return to the House of Commons of the candidate who would put up the strongest opposition to that Government.

I called to see Sir John at the Midland Hotel, Bradford, saying that I was a Socialist, but that, owing to the peculiar political situation, I had decided to support him. His cold face broke into smiles and he asked me if I were willing to sign a statement to that effect and go on to his platform. I told him I would do so on condition that I was allowed to make it clear that I was not a Liberal, but a Socialist, and that at the General Election I should vote Socialist. He agreed, and was very affable, and talked about his father, who was a Congregational minister and said that he himself was still a Congregationalist. His defeat did not exhaust his appreciation; for a few months later at Christmas he sent me a large turkey. But the taste of the turkey soon vanished.

For three weeks I addressed meetings all over the constituency, and met a number of the Liberal leaders. Runciman came to my manse one evening but did not impress me: I should say he was well-fitted for the part he played in Czechoslovakia in 1938. I met Simon several times, each time to like him less. No man was so big a disaster in British politics as he.

3

It was during my Ravensthorpe ministry that I became deeply interested in art, for I became friendly with an art-dealer in Bradford, one of the most original men I have ever met. He saved me from Puritan cant. Addicted to bouts of heavy drinking when he neglected all his responsibilities, in his cups he talked profound and brilliant philosophy. I felt a deep kinship with him. He had a wonderful circle of friends —poets, artists, novelists—among whom he shone by a light of his own. One night my friend introduced me to Jacob Kraemer, the Jewish artist, once known as the leader of the school of Primitives in English art. As a result I spent a good deal of time with Kraemer in his Leeds studio, watching him at work, which was an education. I got to know a little about colour-mixtures, about line-drawing and perspective. I met there, too, many of the younger artists and absorbed their talk, mostly of a rebellious character. They were particularly in rebellion against the New English Art Club. This new world was as remote from the church as the moon from the earth. It accentuated my sense of isolation from religion.

I acquired the silly delusion of possessing the "artistic temperament". What that meant I never discovered, but it seemed to carry with it licence to disown responsibilities. In practice it put a premium upon subjectivism. You did a thing only if you felt like it, and if you felt it: that was its justification. The effect upon me was altogether bad. It gave me the excuse I needed for alienation from my church and people. Moreover, it fostered my pride. It made me feel superior to kindly, decent people who, whatever their narrowness and provincialism, fulfilled their obligations in life, which was more than I was doing, and more than most of the artists I met were doing.

I was cured homoeopathically. Once I spent a week in London with Kraemer and saw Bohemia on the inside and found it not at all a pretty sight. Among the experiences of that week was a meeting with Jacob Epstein, which started at the Café Royal and ended at his studio. He was altogether different from the rabble, a strong, disciplined man of genius. He had just completed his famous figure of Christ, which was on exhibition at the Leicester Galleries. I was very greatly impressed by this work and pinned up an enlarged photograph of it in the vestibule of my church. I also preached a sermon on it—to the great disgust of some members of my congregation, but to the indifference of the majority. Epstein had said he wanted to portray a real man, not a god. His work was a reaction to the Renan conception of a sunny romantic, feminine, futile Christ, and not without great value.

I was finally cured of my "temperament" by the loss of a hundred pounds. A member of Kraemer's circus, with whom I was very intimate, asked me to guarantee him at his bank for a hundred pounds. I did—and lost. What I got out of that guarantee were a few pictures—and the smashing of an illusion. One hundred pounds was a mountain of money which I could not afford. The Bank insisted on its payment, and I was involved in acute money difficulties which certainly did not help me in my ministerial work.

All this experience, however, had a credit side, which was

77

that it brought me to the study of art and did much to cultivate my taste and extend the scope of my reading. I read the history of art and followed its development, and for a time spent the greater part of my holidays at the National Gallery, the Tate Gallery and the Louvre. And through painting I came to architecture, which has ever been a source of great joy to me. Later on I became happy in the friendship of Walter Gropius and Erwin Gutkind, leaders of the Bauhaus Movement in Germany, until the coming of the barbarians drove them from their native land.

As the reader will see, my real life at Ravensthorpe was not in the church, but outside it, evidence, amongst other things, of a restless, questing mind. In a blind way I was seeking a religion co-terminous with the whole of life. But in my search religious work was divorced from cultural activity, and cultural activity from religion. I lived in separate zones, which never met. My artistic and literary friends wondered why I remained in the church, and my congregation increasingly wondered the same thing, feeling, quite rightly, that I was becoming less and less their minister. We no longer understood one another. It became obvious that the only possible thing was to move to some other church. Through my friendship with the Rev. Herbert Brook, I was invited to preach at Hawkeshead Street Congregational Church, Southport. I must have made an impression; for a few weeks later I was asked to preach again, this time "with a view" to the possibility of becoming the minister. I went a second time. After the evening service, I was interviewed by the deacons who asked me all sorts of questions. Amongst them was one about my attitude to war, which I answered in no uncertain manner. In due course I received a unanimous invitation. I ended my ministry at Ravensthorpe on the last Sunday of September, 1922, five years of frustration, defeat and sorrow. I started my ministry at Southport on the first Sunday in October.

The year before this, however, I had married. Among

my friends in the No-Conscription Fellowship, was Edith Firth, whose parents made their home a place of mental and spiritual restfulness for me. Her mother was a charming woman, very intelligent and spiritually minded. Her father, Arthur Firth, a shy, retiring man, but a keen worker in the Labour movement, and a great friend of Fred Jowett, for many years Labour M.P. for Bradford. Artists, writers, hunger-marchers, pioneers of social revolution and leaders of many schools of thought, were constant visitors or guests in this household. Edith had spent her childhood and youth in such an atmosphere, and developed a great love of books. She became a teacher and was teaching in a girls' school at Bradford when we married. Like her father she was quiet and retiring, but became an understanding and able help-mate to me, one on whom I knew I could always depend. She seconded me in my desire to move to Southport, but as it turned out, the new ministry was a greater disaster than my Ravensthorpe ministry. It was bound to be so, for I had no Gospel, and my disintegration proceeded apace. On the small, microscopic plane of individual life, the same process was taking place in me as was happening in the macrocosm of society. Southport brought me a long step forward towards the great disaster of my life.

4

Hawkeshead Street Church was a pleasing little building in the Gothic style, with a seating capacity of just over 400. Its membership was about 100. My morning congregation averaged thirty to forty, my evening congregation eighty to a hundred. We had a Sunday School of about sixty. As is the rule in seaside towns, the Sunday School was less than the Church membership. In the winter months, we had a Young People's Fellowship of twenty-five to thirty young people from sixteen to sixty. And on Wednesday evenings we held the mid-week devotional service. On Sunday afternoons, apart from the school, there was a Men's Bible Class which I attended regularly. One of its members in particular, the late Alfred Cobham, was a most remarkable man, a working painter and decorator, who had attended W.E.A. classes from their inception. In recognition of his work, Cambridge granted him its honorary Master of Arts degree—the only one given to a working man still following his trade. He was a great fellow and most lovable, a born rebel and an eternal child. He regarded his academic degree as a joke. But Southport took it very seriously, which Alfred regarded as a greater joke. In 1927, he committed suicide, a real grief to me, for he was a very good friend.

The social composition of the church membership was, as a Marxist would say, *petit-bourgeois*. Very *petit-bourgeois*. Friends assured me that I, a Socialist, was making a mistake to go to Southport. It was like sending a prophet to Jerusalem. But with incurable optimism, I refused to listen. I felt sure I would succeed. In the circumstances, success was impossible, for my church was really a *rentier* church: about half its membership was made up of retired cotton merchants (large and small), retired trades people and retired nondescripts. The other half consisted of business men, tradesmen, and a minority of working people and boarding-house keepers. How could I succeed? But I was enthusiastic and liked the church and people; even at the end of my ministry six years later, when my work collapsed like a house of cards, I did not lose regard for my most determined opponents.

When I left Ravensthorpe, I had determined to confine my activities to the church and the corporate church life of the town; events willed otherwise. For three years and a half I stuck to my decision; but in 1926, the General Strike and the Miners' Lock-out carried me away as in a flood. I shall come to that later.

One result of the deflation of my "artistic temperament" was to drive me back to theology and philosophy, to which

I brought a comparatively fresh mind. For nearly two years theological reading had been nil. When I got down to it, I discovered a zest for it I had not felt for years. During my first winter I made a systematic study of the history of the doctrine of the Atonement, using for the purpose Franks' work on the subject, also reading round about the subject a great deal. I became a subscriber to Boots' Library and read voraciously. One can waste a lot of time with new books, though there is a strong argument for ministerial familiarity with contemporary writers. Ministers ought to know what their own time is thinking. I also undertook systematic reading of Russian literature, particularly Dostoievsky, Tolstoy, Turgenev and Tchekov.

From all this the reader will gather, quite correctly, that I was not idle. Mornings and late evenings were almost invariably given to reading. Blessed with a tough constitution, I can burn the candle at both ends; a foolish thing to do, it is said, but on the whole my experience is otherwise. After the day's meeting or visiting, I would settle down to four or five hours' reading before going to bed.

Throughout that first winter, things seemed to go very well, except for complaints from some of the old people that my preaching was a bit socialist. I was ill at ease about the mid-week service, which was attended by no more than ten or a dozen people, mostly elderly women, very worthy but not exactly dynamic. How to revive it was my problem. It was a miniature Sunday service, except that it was held in the church schoolroom, and that one of the deacons used to take the prayer. I determined to do something about it.

During the summer I planned a connected series of addresses to cover the winter from October to April. The subject was "Prophets Ancient and Modern", beginning with Amos and ending with Bernard Shaw. Into the series came St. Paul, St. Augustine, Dante, Savonarola, St. Francis of Assisi, Luther; and among the moderns, Marx, Robert Owen, Keir Hardie, Dostoievsky, Francis Thompson and others: a mixed lot. I drew upon my reading of years, and also read specially for it. I found the preparation very informing and stimulating. I learnt a good deal. I wrote out the addresses, word for word.

When I put the idea to my deacons' meeting and suggested a printed syllabus of the whole series, they agreed with enthusiasm. I decided to visit every member of my congregation with the object of persuading them to make a point of attending this series of week-night services. To each I gave a copy of the syllabus, I got promises from most of them to attend.

Judged by statistics, that was the most successful thing I ever did in the ministry. The attendance jumped from a dozen to between sixty and seventy. The church schoolroom was packed out week after week. Interest was maintained almost to the end of the course; it flagged a little, but revived. For the last lecture on Shaw we were crowded to suffocation. I never enjoyed anything in my work so much; the most encouraging thing about it was the number of young people that attended.

We felt the backwash in our Sunday evening services, with increased congregations. I copied a practice of the famous Dr. R. F. Horton of Hampstead. On the last Sunday evening of each month, I delivered what I called a Monthly Lecture on a subject of topical interest. A breath of life stirred in the church throughout the winter.

I was looking forward with a good deal of heart to the following winter's work, and set about the preparation of another series of addresses on "The Search for Eternal Life". The syllabus was printed as before, and I did the delivery and the visitation. Then, like a bolt from the blue, I was stricken with rheumatism. One morning I awoke with acute pains in my shoulder and legs. I could hardly move. The doctor called it rheumatism, which, of course, could mean anything. Whatever was it? I had to stay in bed, where I lay for six weeks. For nearly three months I was out of my pulpit, and when I did start preaching again, I moved with such pain and difficulty that I could do no more than the two services on Sundays. I couldn't walk without a stick, and then at a snail's pace. It was not for two years that I resumed my full week, when the week-night services were back again in the rut.

Meanwhile I was persisting with treatment which varied considerably. I tried dieting, and had a course of injections, all to no purpose. Movement was an agony. I got very depressed. At last it was decided that I should try a course of hydropathic treatment. Southport bristled with Hydros. I went as an external patient to one which had a Free Church clientèle. There was this to be said about it: at the beginning of the treatment I was able to walk, though only just; at the end I was paralysed, and had to be wheeled about in a bath-chair! This experience was one long misery, the worst aspect of it being the involuntary companionship of old men, and being compelled to listen day after day to the retailing of the details of their physical ailments—old men with an abundance of wealth and egotism. Mostly good Nonconformists, for the Hydro especially catered for them.

Whilst it would not be true to say that I went to pieces, it was very nearly true, and without the devotion and ceaseless attention of Edith and her mother, it almost certainly would have been true. I could not get rid of the desperate feeling that my life was fated to fail. In the preceding winter I had found promise of great possibilities, which had been very effectually squashed. The situation revealed in me a grave weakness of character, which I refused to face. I had suppressed awareness of it, but resolutely resisted its emergence into full consciousness, so that I became a prey to frequently recurring moods of moroseness and depression.

Being physically unable to perform the duties of the pastorate, I was psychically and spiritually isolated from the church. In a different form my Ravensthorpe experience was being repeated. I spent the summer of 1925 mostly on my back. When I went out it was in the bath-chair. I retreated into an abstract world of my own.

Except in my worst moods, I kept up my reading. But even that had become difficult. One piece of good I did accomplish, for I got hold of Frazer's *Golden Bough* and was fascinated. This led to a prolonged course of reading in anthropology and comparative religion. From that was but a step to the psychology of religion. I acquired a general idea of what was being thought and written in these fields.

Towards the end of 1925, there occurred an incident which was to influence my future very much. A young man came to see me about his wedding; he wanted to get married on Boxing Day. Though he was a complete stranger, we at once became very close friends. He confessed that the reason he wanted me to perform the wedding ceremony was that he had heard one of his work-mates at the Vulcan Engineering Works refer to me as a Bolshie. Being a bit of a Bolshie himself, his curiosity was quickened, so he came to Hawkeshead Street to be married. I carried out the ceremony with great difficulty.

From that meeting there followed a whole train of events which I shall relate in the next chapter. Meanwhile, I was getting about a bit better, though still suffering great pain. I had discarded the bath-chair—temporarily, as it proved—and reverted to the use of walking-sticks. One day my new engineer friend asked me if I was prepared to talk to a few of his work-mates. He warned me that they were extreme Socialists and had no use for the church; but they would like to have an argument with me. So early in the new year (1926), I arranged a series of meetings on Tuesday evenings at the church schoolroom, at which I was to give a short address, to be followed by questions and discussion. The deacons were not enthusiastic, though they did grant the use of the schoolroom. That proved to be the first definite rift, which was to widen into an unbridgeable gulf.

I was keen on these meetings. For the first time since I

had left home for the University, I made contact with convinced trade unionists and socialists. Those meetings grew from about half a dozen to an attendance of over thirty, and I became personally friendly with most of the men. A few started coming to the Sunday services. I set myself out in my preaching to attract and hold them. At once I sensed an incipient hostility in the attitude of the deacons and the older members of the church, vague and ill-defined, but most certainly there.

The meetings continued for several months, until at last—so it seemed—I became a daily topic of conversation at the Vulcan works. The tiny trickle of men into the Sunday evening services increased. My preaching became more definitely and constantly political. This was the situation when an event which convulsed the national life blew both myself and the church clean out of out established routine.

On May the first, 1926, the miners of Great Britain were locked out by the employers. The owners were determined both to reduce wages and to extend the working-day of seven hours to eight. The Trade Union Congress had promised to declare a General Strike if the miners were attacked. So on May the first, the long-talked of, the long-dreaded, General Strike was declared, and hundreds of thousands of workers downed tools in defence of the miners of Great Britain. May the first, 1926! It was the fatal date in my personal history.

CHAPTER VI

RELIGIOUS COLLAPSE

THE MINERS' LOCK-OUT acted upon me with explosive force. It came as a kind of new religious awakening. I am still certain of that. My chief concern when I left Ravensthorpe had been to do well, to succeed in a worldly sense, to keep out of trouble or rows, to give a minimum of offence. Whilst all these objectives may be laudable, they are spiritually deadly if put first. By imperceptible stages I arrived at a position when the institution meant more than the Gospel. I believe that my rheumatic attack was part of the mercy of God; for my illness violently threw me out of that position. When the lock-out happened, I needed something to sweep me out of my miserable, bourgeois concern for security and popularity—something big and clean and explosive. When the miners came out I never hesitated for a second: I had found what I wanted. My barque was lifted from a paddling pool to brave and stormy waters. It was like magic to my rheumatism. I was suddenly almost as if well again. Every moment of my day became invested with significance. As I look back I can see that I made many mistakes and was guilty of grave errors throughout the struggle; but fundamentally I was right to respond in the way I did, to hazard everything in one throw.

I felt the pull of the miners' struggle because I had been a miner and knew the hardship of their lot. I felt a class loyalty, which most certainly has its place. I was thus acutely conscious of the injustice which the coal owners proposed to inflict upon their workers. At their old game—these Junkers of British industry! A. J. Cook's slogan, "Not a cent off the pay, not a second on the day", fired every nerve in my body. I was overwhelmingly certain that the church ought to support the miners in their struggle, through thick and thin. As I put it, in the first sermon I preached on the issue, "The miners are altogether right and the owners are altogether wrong". That was how I saw it. So I burnt my bridges, and jumped with both feet down on the side of the miners. I did what I could to influence the church to take the same action.

A preliminary "spar" with a few of my church officials— an affair of outposts, so to speak—showed the set of events and their development. One day, after it had become certain that the miners were going to fight, I met one of the church officers in the street, and we fell to discussing the prospective struggle. He made it clear where his sympathies lay, and I, very aggressively, made it clear where mine were. From that day, hostility arose. My determination stiffened.

I

On the Monday of the first week of the General Strike, my engineer friend asked if I was going to preach on the matter. If I would let him have the subject of next Sunday's sermon, he said, he would have it announced at the workers' mass meetings, which were being held at one of the largest halls in Southport. It was too good a chance to miss. Every night 1,500 men and women were packed together. I gave him the subject—Christianity and the Miners' Claim.

On the following Thursday, my senior deacon came to see me. He was a good man, a bit mercurial and unconventional, but very human and likeable—not at all a typical deacon. He was a very good friend to me to the day of his death. All through the subsequent trouble, he was utterly staunch in his support of me. I am glad to pay him this tribute. He called, very perturbed at the news that I was going to preach on the Strike. He impressed upon me that he spoke as my friend. His concern was for me. He begged me not to preach on the Strike because, he said, he knew that it would make for trouble and divide the church. People were already saying that I wasn't preaching the Gospel. If I took the line I proposed, it would give them just the handle they needed. I was adamant—indeed I was macadamant (if I may coin a word). Nothing would deter me. It was then that I began to realize that this would probably mean my resignation. I became reckless. "Since I shall have to walk the plank," I said to myself, "I'll walk it as a giant, not as a pigmy." So in the preparation of my sermon, I did not mince my words.

Sunday came. I set off for the evening service a little earlier than usual, hobbling along on my walking sticks. As I came within sight of the church, I saw, to my amazement, a long queue. I felt transported. When I got inside the building a few people were looking for dusters to clean up the gallery, which had not been opened for many years. Long before the music started, the church was packed out. It was with difficulty that I made my way to the pulpit.

I shall never forget that service. The congregation was made up overwhelmingly of men—most of them striking on behalf of their fellow-workers. I felt moved to the very roots of my being. The air was electric. Anything might happen. The singing was full-throated, with that determined boom of the bass. I was keyed up to a painful pitch of tension and restraint. That was the atmosphere in which I preached. Words came pouring out in a molten rush. For the first time in my experience, a congregation punctuated my utterance with a periodical "hear, hear", and at the end broke into applause. That, I confess, jarred upon me, as somehow out of place. But it was a wonderful service. "There! What do you think?" I asked the church secretary. "It will never last," he answered. "No," I replied, "you are determined to see that it won't last."

The whole affair went to my head, and deprived me of every vestige of judgment. The half-conscious assumption that lay embedded in my mind that the main job of the church was really to establish Socialism suddenly became determinative. It aggressively inspired my thinking and preaching. It disguised itself religiously as bringing the Kingdom of God to earth, which was the mission of Jesus. The sole purpose of His life had been to overthrow Roman civilization and establish a co-operative commonwealth: it was for this that the vested interests of Roman Imperialism and Jewish institutional religion crucified Him. So, in fighting for the miners and for a socialist order, I was doing directly what Christ had done. This idea came to occupy my mind to the exclusion of every other thought. For two years I literally preached nothing else. All texts led to the miners and socialism.

At one stroke I was swept away from any pastoral relation to the members of the church and congregation. I came to think of them as obstructive, reactionary and blind. My energies and affections were concentrated on the new people who attended the services. I idealized them. These were the "outsiders" whom the churches had failed to attract. And lo! here I was attracting them! These were the people who were seriously concerned about real things, they whom the pettiness of the churches had repelled. I must appeal to these people—who were all of socialist and trade-union sympathies. I must get to know them, look after them, nurse them into church membership. "The old guard" were hopeless, and to try to convert them would be waste of time. Anyhow, they were determined to scotch the new development. Open and violent hostility between myself and the church officers blew up, which drove me more and more to the newcomers.

I became the slave of my social gospel. No preacher ever trimmed his sails to the prejudices of the wealthy membership more than I trimmed my sails to that new socialist incursion to my church. Of course I should have indignantly denied any such indictment had it been made. My self-deception was perfect and complete. What I was doing, in my own mind, was upholding genuine Christianity. I preached exactly what my new congregation wanted and expected. I expressed in the pulpit what they themselves believed and desired. I preached party politics—Labour-party politics—in a religious guise. Between May and November, 1926, there was not a single sermon in which some aspect or another of the miners' struggle was not dealt with. And between November, 1926, and April, 1928, when I resigned, my preaching dealt only with social and political issues—from the socialist angle.

I had suddenly become what I had longed to be, a "popular" preacher; but I was the slave of my popularity. Sunday after Sunday, I had to live up to what my new congregation expected of me. I had to give capitalism hell—and so I did. I had to reveal the heroism and virtues of the working-class—and so I did. I had to be strong, smashing and sensational—and I so was. That congregation would have tolerated nothing else. One teaspoonful of the genuine New Testament Gospel would have sent them packing.

"Put not your trust in princes," not even in the sprawling, mass, collective prince known as "the people". I was popular for a brief season because I toed the popular line. Once a preacher makes the preference of his congregation his guiding principle, he is done for, though nothing is more difficult to guard against. Self-deception is the supreme clerical vice. How easy it is to persuade oneself that one is preaching truth, when all one is doing is "rationalizing" the prejudices of a congregation, especially if one's income depends upon that congregation! Now I see clearly that that is what I did in those Southport years.

One other thing I have come to understand about this period in my development: that the opposition of "the old guard" in my church was giving expression to the deep and precious feeling that the Gospel was being perverted. Much of that opposition was bitter, petty and visionless, because the people who opposed were human, very human. But in spite of that, it was intuitively right. Those good, narrow-minded, conventional Congregationalists scented a deep heresy in my preaching and activity; they became aware that something infinitely vital was being jettisoned. Under the circumstances, they were utterly right in bringing about my resignation. It was a service to the church and the Gospel.

2

The startling increase in the evening congregation which I have recorded maintained itself with varying fluctuations for two years, when I terminated my ministry. On special occasions—i.e., when we "billed" the services—the church was crowded. We registered a net increase in church membership of over 200. On Sunday evenings the church was always comfortably full, at the least, and quite often packed. It caused a sensation in Southport. In that complacent, conservative town, I became known as "the Bolshie parson". The Southport Press did me a good turn without intending to do anything of the kind. Whenever, for instance, I made a public speech, the *Visitor* or *Guardian* fastened on some statement, usually torn from its context, and mercilessly castigated me. Of course it was cheap publicity. I became a curiosity, and people came to the church just to hear the Bolshie. For a long time, the correspondence columns of the papers were filled with angry letters, attacking and defending me. I was for a time, perhaps, the best-hated and best-loved figure in the town. As the Free Churches proceeded to ostracize me, the local Labour Movement took me to its breast. Some of its leaders, however, resented the newcomer who was monopolizing the limelight and edging them into darkness. But as long as it lasted it was magnificent.

Within a very short time I was snowed under with invitations to address miners' meetings all over the Lancashire coal-field. In spite of the pain of my rheumatism, which, despite my high spirits, still compelled me to hobble, I accepted as many of these invitations as I could. Arriving at the meeting-place, I was lifted on to the platform. Leaning on the table I proceeded to deliver my speech. I became the object of much sentimental sympathy, especially from the women. When the chairman praised me for my zeal in coming to speak under such a handicap, and compared me to Philip Snowden, I purred within.

Very soon I met A. J. Cook, the tempestuous leader of the miners. Idolized by them, he was execrated by the middle-classes. I shall not attempt to discuss his leadership of the miners in their great struggle, except to say that he was a man of transparent honesty and burning sincerity. It was for these qualities that the miners trusted and loved him. There was not a trace of careerism in him. I saw a great deal of him during the struggle and afterwards in London. Some of his oratorical performances were astonishing. I was speaking with him on one occasion at a Liverpool meeting—or rather I was supposed to speak. There was an audience of about five thousand. He orated for two and a half hours—a tornado of words. At the end he collapsed. He did this three or four times a week for six months. Arthur Cook was morally a great man. There was a good deal of the prophet in him. He was driven by a daemon. Long before he died he suffered a deep disillusionment which he did his best to hide. The miners have had many able leaders, but never one more trustworthy.

Practically my whole time during that summer (1926) was given to political and social agitation for the miners. Every night I was not away from Southport I addressed open-air meetings on the sands. I was actively engaged in organizing support for them. Every Sunday evening we made retiring collections at my church. I helped too with a committee for billeting miners' children in various homes. Imperceptibly I was being drawn into purely political activity. In spite of myself, I was pitchforked into the leadership of the local movement, which caused much heart-burning.

From all this the reader will gather that I lived a rather stormy, hectic existence. One of the by-products of my agitation was the complete cure of my rheumatism. It disappeared like magic, as suddenly as it had come, in August. I had decided to go to North Wales for a week's rest and left Southport hobbling on two sticks. Two days after my arrival I threw the sticks away. In less than a week I had climbed Snowdon. This is the sober fact. When I returned to Southport my friends could not believe in the transformation. My doctor was puzzled—and delighted. He then impressed upon me that I should always wear woollens next to my skin and must never get my feet wet. I laughed at him. I said that whatever I did, I should never suffer from rheumatism again. I never have. That was over thirty years ago, and I've not had as much as a twinge. I have no explanation. I record it as a fact.

My political activities naturally increased the support and loyalty of the new adherents to the church, but equally naturally alienated the older members more and more. Relations became very bad. There was constant bitter friction. I came to regard the church officials as enemies, and they repaid the compliment. I got busy among the newcomers and urged upon them the duty of joining the church, which they did in sufficient numbers to secure a majority in my support at church meetings. The secretary and treasurer resigned, and these and other offices were filled by my supporters. So far as numbers went we were secure, but finance proved to be a different matter. Most of the older members either reduced or ended their subscriptions, which had been generous. In place of their pounds and shillings, the pennies of the greater numbers were an inadequate compensation, and so the church began to accumulate debt which in a short time assumed serious proportions. In the end it defeated us.

Meanwhile, my ministry had degenerated into politics, and my church had become a Labour church. So the local Labour Party invited me to contest one of the wards at the November municipal elections in 1926. After a great deal of hesitation I consented. I was launched upon a political career. It proved to be dust and ashes.

3

The Sussex ward in Southport had been held by the Conservatives for a period of about fifteen years, and latterly their candidate's return had been unopposed. It was felt that my popularity among the working section of the people gave a chance—an outside chance—to win the seat for Labour. I was nominated to oppose Councillor Clayton, a strong candidate. He was one of the founders of the famous Southport Flower Show and a director of the Southport Football Club: he had been in undisturbed possession of the seat for about fifteen years. As I learnt afterwards, the betting among the Tories was simply about the size of the majority by which I was to be beaten.

I got the ward committee together and impressed upon them the necessity of a thorough canvass, which is of much greater importance than public meetings. So I proposed a double canvass. I undertook a personal canvass of every voter. The canvassers proper were to report to me their difficult, wavering cases, whom I would then specially visit. About five weeks before the election, I began work, during which I visited every house in the ward. I was at it sixteen hours a day in all weathers. Except for absent voters, I spoke to every elector in the ward. On the eve of the poll, when we were sizing up the results of our five weeks' work, I worked out that, according to the canvass, I should get a majority of 200. I concluded that the actual majority would be about 100 by simply writing off 50 per cent. of the promises. My actual majority was 99.

The result was a first-class local sensation. The Labour people went wild with delight. With only three motor-cars, we firmly shepherded our people to the polls. At the end of polling day, when it had poured with rain, I had become a Socialist councillor—the one and only Socialist in a Borough Council of 62 Liberals and Conservatives. For one year, I enjoyed a lonely eminence. My friend, the editor of the *Southport Journal*, reported my speeches in the Council Chamber almost verbatim.

But as a Socialist, I could do nothing, except propaganda. I could not even get my motions seconded. Let me give one example. In the winter of 1926, many Town Councils made grants to the Miners' Relief Funds. I moved that the Southport Borough Council should make a grant of £1,000 to the Fund. I spoke for about twenty minutes—from the heart. Many of the councillors said it was a moving, powerful speech, but not powerful enough to move any of them even to second my motion, so that it could not even be discussed. I was listened to in silence—then the council passed on to the next business. This happened every time I moved a motion. Inevitably this induced a sense of futility and irresponsibility, so that I simply used the Council Chamber as a platform to address Socialist propaganda to the outside public.

Only on one occasion did I win approval from my Liberal and Tory fellow-councillors. The council had spent £60,000 on a new bathing-pool. I had opposed it on the ground that the £60,000 should be spent on houses for the Southport workers rather than in adding to the amenities for visitors. My opposition had had as much effect as the chirping of a sparrow in a storm. The bathing-pool was proceeded with and completed. The question was should it be open on Sunday. Of course, everybody except me, a Congregational minister, opposed the Sunday opening. To the general surprise, and to the fury of the local Free Church Council, I supported it. I let myself go. I said some stinging things about the "Nonconformist conscience". I fear it was a vengeful speech. But it made me momentarily popular inside the Council Chamber. Of course, to the Free Churches of the town, I was long past redemption, but that never worried me.

The real work of a Town Council is done in committee, in which I took my full share. I served on the Gas Committee (a most appropriate appointment!), the Highways, the Libraries and Arts, and the Housing Sub-Committee. I was kept very busy. A Borough councillor even then could hardly call his soul his own. Never had I less time for reading and personal pursuits. I was at the beck and call of every one in my ward who had a grievance: men wanting jobs; council employees with wage or work complaints; municipal tenants who were dissatisfied with their houses; people wanting houses; vested interests with an axe to grind, etc. My day was a procession of interruptions. Reading was confined to snatches.

However, it was a valuable experience. For the first time I came into human contact with political opponents; I found them kindly and decent. The experience taught me to see through the labels to the reality behind. I am afraid I should make an indifferent revolutionary. Southport made me too much aware of the virtues of my enemies and the vices of my allies ever to be ruthless enough. I also learnt that political narrowness is by no means a monopoly of opponents, which makes it impossible for me to be a good party-man.

Elected for three years, I resigned at the end of my second year, when I had to be absent from the town for long periods, and so could not fulfil the duties of my office. When I sent in my resignation I was surprised to receive from the town clerk a letter stating that, since my resignation was not accompanied by the sum of one shilling, he could not accept it. Truth to tell, I was tremendously relieved to become a private individual once more.

4

Early in the new year (1927), officers had been appointed in the church from the Labour and Socialist incursion. I had practically a new diaconate and church committee, who were, of course, in sympathy with my attitude. They were all thoroughly secularist. The test of membership was not religious; it was social. In fact it was socialist. At any rate only socialists joined the church. The question I put to intending members was: Do you believe in fighting for the Kingdom of God, i.e., a new social order, based upon Socialism? We printed the following card:

Hawkeshead Street Congregational Church.

Minister

Rev. D. R. Davies.

Services 10.30 a.m. and 6.30 p.m.

When any Church will inscribe over its altar, as its sole qualification for membership, the Saviour's condensed statement of the substance of both Law and Gospel:

Thou shalt love the Lord thy God with all thy heart, and with all thy soul, and with all thy mind, and thy neighbour as thyself

that Church will I join with all my heart and with all my soul.

Abraham Lincoln.

This Church stands instinctively for the Social Gospel, for the application of Christian Principles in Industry, Politics and International Affairs. In pursuit of that vision and ideal which Jesus called the Kingdom of God, the Church, during the Miners' Lock-Out of 1926, loyally supported the Miners' Cause by material contributions, by prayer and sympathy. We give a hearty welcome to all to attend our services.

The result was, though I did not realize it at the time, that there were admitted into church membership scores of people who cared less than nothing for the New Testament

G 97

Gospel, and who were innocent of any fundamental Christian experience. In effect, the church degenerated into a branch of the Labour Party. The services were predominantly political, hymns, prayers, the lesson (frequently read from outside the Bible) and the sermon, especially the sermon. Since the main purpose of Jesus was to create a new social order, I used to say, the true business of the church was to agitate against Capitalism, which was the chief obstacle to the new order. That was the task of the church, *if—IF—Christ's mission was to create a new social order on earth, if by Kingdom of God He meant merely a new civilization.* What I did was to draw, simply and directly, the essential logical conclusion from that idea.

Let me point out, in passing, what seems to me the truth, that my ministry in 1926–8 was the *reductio ad absurdum* of the Congregational Church practice, bringing to utter futility the theory that the church is constituted by the local congregation. So long as I could get the support of a congregation, there was no authority in Congregationalism to call me to account. I converted a Christian church into a political organization—and remained Congregational. I was sincere, of course, but I had betrayed the Gospel. With neither authority nor dogma, as my case proved, the Gospel (and the Church) are defenceless against the vagaries and moods of the individual.

So it happened that our monthly church meetings were given over mainly to the discussion of political issues. I give two examples. In 1927, when the Disarmament Conference was being prepared, Litvinov, who was then the Soviet Commissar for Foreign Affairs, tabled a startling proposal for complete and immediate disarmament, which the democratic diplomats and statesmen of the West regarded as a tasteless joke. But we ardent, deluded Christian Socialists took it very seriously. We discussed it hopefully and passed a resolution urging Great Britain to give it support, sending a copy to the Foreign Secretary! In 1927 also, when Britain despatched soldiers and sailors to Shanghai in defence of British lives and property against Chinese revolts, we passed a resolution condemning the action and urging the return of the Treaty ports to China. We sent a copy of that resolution also to the Foreign Secretary. When we sent a copy to Dr. Sidney Berry, secretary of the Congregational Union, he replied to say he was glad to observe that we were concerning ourselves with big issues!

In addition to all this, I did a considerable amount of political speaking outside the church in various parts of Lancashire. I suppose it would be true to say that I was in great demand as a speaker. My Celtic, romantic tendency for extreme statements was being stimulated by circumstances. In a speech at Ainsdale on the Labour Party platform, I stated that I had been accused of being an extreme Socialist, and declared it was the duty of every decent man to be extreme in a civilization that imposed poverty on the masses. The local Conservative candidate savagely attacked me in a letter to the Southport *Visitor*, so I promptly challenged him to a public debate. He sportingly accepted. It was arranged that we should debate the question, "Has Capitalism failed to provide a Good Life for the Masses?" at the Cambridge Hall (the largest in the town) under an independent chairman. The hall was packed at an admission fee of sixpence, and feeling ran high. The candidate was a halting speaker, while in my torrential manner I had no difficulty in getting an overwhelmingly positive answer to the question. Afterwards we became good friends, for, as he said, he hadn't realized I was a "gentleman"!

This debate brought me an invitation from the Lancaster Labour Party to succeed Fenner Brockway as Labour candidate. Within a few weeks of my acceptance, the sitting member was elevated to the peerage and I was faced with a by-election. There were two other candidates. I had a hectic campaign of three weeks, during which I addressed over a hundred and fifty meetings. Never have I worked harder, from early morning to midnight—meetings, interviews and canvassing. Needless to say, I was defeated by a large and enthusiastic majority, the election being won for the Liberal by the dramatic intervention of Lloyd George himself. "He came, saw and conquered." In the following year, I happened to be present at the International Sheep Dog Trials at Llandudno, when Lloyd George was distributing the prizes. I introduced myself to him as a man who had a grudge. He stared at me. When I told him what it was—that he had deprived me of a Parliamentary seat in Lancaster!—his face broke into smiles; the recollection gave him pleasure.

5

Things were rapidly coming to a head within the church. Our debt grew larger and larger. Another factor was growing disunity. Being a Labour church, we reflected the enmities, jealousies and disputes of the local movement. Many of the congregation left. I had become identified with one section of the Labour Party and so became the target for the hostility of other sections. At that time, the party at Southport was disaffiliated on the Communist issue, which had split not only the party but also my church. The bitterness engendered was worse than that displayed by my old guard religious opponents and I suddenly felt a revulsion for the whole situation and decided to resign. Not only had I grown weary of that church, but I had become tired of the ministry altogether. The church, I concluded, was an enemy to be fought. So I resigned my ministry at the end of April, 1928, after two years of public controversy, bitterness and storm.

There remained, however, about fifty or sixty of a loyal following; they got together and suggested that we should start a real Labour Church. They urged me to act as minister, which I consented to do. We hired a hall in the town and conducted services at 6.30—just the one service—on Sunday evenings.

Incredible as this may sound this "church" lasted just over a year. I made no pretence of being anything but a mere politician and agitator. I delivered political speeches every Sunday evening. A marked and rapid disintegration took place in myself. Deep down I realized the miserable futility of the whole business. I knew that what I was doing was hopeless, but I carried on—because it was my only source of income. What could I do? I dreaded facing the prospect of poverty and insecurity once again. I came to feel very bitter towards not only the church but the Labour Movement. The effect upon my character was deplorable. My idealism evaporated and I lived from day to day. I lost my enthusiasm, even though I still continued to speak and agitate. I became indifferent. I was frequently absent from Southport for long periods on speaking campaigns. But the spirit that once inspired me had fled.

The Labour church dwindled away to a mere handful of personal friends, who were much kinder to me than I deserved. I finally determined to finish with it. After the General Election of 1929, when I supported several Labour candidates, I shook the dust of Southport from my feet.

6

To summarize my ministerial career, which started in September, 1917, and ended in April, 1928—for my year's experiment as leader of a Labour church was a mere miserable and futile epilogue—it was ten years and a half of preaching a modernist gospel, at the end of which I had managed, in my own mind, to separate Christianity from the Church and to identify it with a movement for social change.

The inherent logic of my position was that Christianity was part of the dynamic movement of the natural man, part of the fundamental striving and goodness of the human being. In ten years the logic of my position had become explicit. The Church had ceased to be indispensable. To me, it had become a hindrance and an enemy. What had happened was that I had telescoped into ten years a process that was operating more slowly in the larger, historic scale of the whole of the Church and the world. Just as the human embryo "recapitulates" the evolutionary past of life, so I anticipated in my ten years the inevitable longer-drawn-out future process of a merely humanist Christianity, the final logic of which is that the Church loses her identity in the natural development of secular society. In ten years I had boxed the compass of an entire historic development. That, I believe, was the inner significance of my years in the ministry: I had come to the conclusion that I could more effectively propagate Christianity through secular movements for social change and reform. I had boarded the same boat as the hundred thousands of secularized souls who to-day indulge in the self-deception of saying that you can be a Christian without going to church—better in fact—that you can worship God in Nature. God becomes more real in a motor-car than when kneeling before the altar.

At the start of my ministry I did have some sort of devotional life, rather thin and shallow, but certainly existing. I "said" prayers at the end of the day. Much more rarely, I entered a church in midweek for prayers. I used to read books of prayers. At one time, I tried to follow a scheme of praying recommended by Dr. Orchard, but without success. The point is that I had some sort of devotional life, pinchbeck though it was.

During the later political years of my ministry, I ceased to pray altogether. I no longer felt the need for prayer. Indeed, I have to record that in the last two years of ministry, 1926–1928, even public prayer was something of a bore. I was thirsting to get to the sermon. My prayers from the pulpit were, in fact, no more than a preface to the sermon. Action was the thing—more wages for the miners, Home Rule for India, nationalization of the banks and heavy industries

—there was your true prayer. In the stress of a political, humanist ministry, my prayer life evaporated.

Another fact I record is that I had become very bitter. I felt great indignation at the very unchristian treatment I had received at the hands of the Christians. Let me make it clear that I am under no illusion now as to what that indignation meant—it was a very effective disguise for my own failure and self-righteousness. But it is, nevertheless, a fact that the Christians were not Christian in their attitude towards me. I had a blisteringly clear eye for their pettiness, but none for my own. I saw myself as a martyr to truth and the Gospel. Had I not preached the very surgical, unpopular truth? And the people had not liked it. So I became bitter. I thought of church people as hypocrites.

I was even more bitter about the local Labour Movement. With the best will in the world and with a great deal more objectivity of spirit now than I could boast in 1928, I am still of the opinion that the leaders of the local movement were riddled with jealousies and strife. Their intolerance of one another was incredible. Each had his or her own following. For a brief hour, I monopolized the limelight—a fact for which I was not forgiven. I felt very much of a martyr. I said to myself, "I have risked unpopularity, I plunged to the support of the miners, I have served the movement as speaker, councillor and Parliamentary candidate, for all of which I am slandered and reviled. What ingratitude!"

I have learnt only too well that people are very human, whether Christian, Socialist or what-not. They are never ideal, least of all myself. Imperfect, mixed, egotistic and vain. What else can be expected of sinful men and women?

In spite of the bleakness of my prospects, I felt immense relief when I resigned. The position had become impossible. For two years I had been the storm-centre of controversy, bickering and strife. To be delivered from it was a blessing. With native buoyancy and optimism, I began to look forward to London. I had finished with the ministry. Nothing,

I felt, would ever induce me to return to it. At one stroke I severed my connection with Congregationalism and dropped out without leaving a trace. I began rosy day-dreams of a new career in journalism. I was going to London as a free-lance. I allowed for a rough time to begin with, but only for a short while. I had plenty of confidence in my power to conquer London editors. Ultimately, I thought, I should become an editor myself. And the amazing thing is that I did. But through what purgatory had I to pass!

So I packed up my belongings, which was chiefly a library of over 3,000 volumes; and my wife went into lodgings. Leaving her and my books behind, but with my fountain pen and my brains, I set out to conquer the capital.

CHAPTER VII

IN THE FAR COUNTRY

I ARRIVED IN London on a lovely dawn one day in late August, 1929, with my fountain pen and £5. In my heart and through my nerves moved deep excitement. London at last! How often had I dreamed of being welcomed by a crowd of people as a celebrated popular preacher in the City Temple, or Westminster Chapel. Here I was, practically penniless, unknown—and forty years old. I was severed from my ministerial past, and, without a trade except that of a miner, faced with the necessity of immediately earning my daily bread. But at that moment I was far from being depressed. I was exhilarated. The chirping of the street sparrows was at least a welcome, and the Euston Road hid its drabness in a haze of romance. I congratulated myself on my freedom and independence. There would be no more deacons' meetings, no more quarrels, and no more bickerings. I would build a new career, and fight for my ideals in a new way. In a mood of sweet optimism I drank a cup of tea at a coffee-stall outside King's Cross station, at about 4.30 a.m. I would first get going as a free-lance journalist, then rent a flat and get my wife down—and everything would be lovely. There is no fantasy to which a late August dawn does not lend encouragement!

After a few days at an appalling little hotel in Guilford Street, I found a cheap room at Streatham. Why I went out so far I cannot now imagine—it must have been in search of cheapness. I believe I paid seven shillings and sixpence a week. I settled in and transported my library from Southport, Edith remaining behind.

One of these first days, I accidentally ran into A. J. Cook the miners' leader. He seemed delighted to see me. I told him the whole story. He was very interested in all I said and held out hopes of something coming my way. He proved to be the only one with the very slightest hope. I had letters of introduction to a number of leading Labour politicians, but I was very quickly cured of the illusion that my work for the movement counted for anything at all. The assistant editor of the *Daily Herald* held out the possibility of a navvy's job for me! Hamilton Fyfe strongly urged me to stick to the ministry on the ground that "it is your line". He failed to understand that it had ceased to be my line. But Arthur Cook said something would have to be done. Labour was then in office and he did his utmost to get me a job of some kind. All to no purpose. Cook's hopes came to nothing. An edge was put on my determination to make good at journalism.

I

In that single room in Streatham, I settled down to writing. Short stories, topical articles, personal paragraphs, articles on politics, economics and philosophy poured from my fountain pen. But in the course of an entire year these efforts brought me the sum of exactly £6 3s. 0d. Of this amount, three guineas were for an article on Sheep Dog Trials as a sport, and the other three pounds for an article on the Suffragette Movement, commissioned by a man who took pity on me, for I never saw or heard anything more of the article.

For three months I haunted Fleet Street like a ghost, buying what seemed to be hundreds of all sorts of periodicals, everything except the religious ones. I never succeeded in getting a single interview with an editor. As a rule, I got no further than the office boy or girl. With unfailing regularity, my MSS. came back with "The Editor regrets . . ." The dream became a nightmare.

That experience certainly tested my fibre, for somehow I

hung on. I realized with brutal clarity the unreality of the religion I had been preaching for ten years, and in that grim, despairing struggle for bread, my theology withered away. I discovered that I had been preaching many things the truth of which I had never tested. This was not my first experience of poverty; but the constant poverty of my childhood and youth was *secure* poverty. I had my father and mother always at my back. Now I was alone, with a wife dependent on me. In the midst of a wealthy civilization I was in the situation of a primitive food-gatherer, literally hunting for his next meal, for next week's rent.

In those first terrible months, clothes, books, art, tobacco vanished from my life. I learnt in my own flesh the fundamental distinction between poverty and insecurity. Nothing so demoralizes and de-humanizes a man as literal, ultimate, definite poverty. It reduces spirit to matter. It forces on him the belief that the most valuable thing in life is a good meal. That is to say, it compels a man to invest a lie with the quality of truth. It is a lie that food is the greatest value of human existence, a monstrous, satanic lie. But if you have no food *that lie becomes true*. You leave the man who suffers it no alternative and deprive him of the very possibility of spiritual growth. I have no hesitation whatsoever in saying that the worst fate any human being can suffer is, *having eaten one meal, to be obsessed straightaway with getting the next*. That plays hell with theology. I have suffered most of the evils and disasters that befall our human lot: the death of my dearest; physical pain; disillusion. But none compares with the horror of ultimate want.

Like thousands of other ministers and clergy, I had glibly uttered the second-hand truths and consolations of religion. But now I learnt what no college or university could possibly have taught me: *that in religion second-hand truth is futile*.

I had preached the availability of God's presence and power in every human situation, however extreme or disastrous. I discovered that it did not work. Having preached

Christ, as St. Paul puts it, I myself was cast away. The God in my soul was useless. The more I looked into myself, the more impossible my situation grew. The things I encountered in myself at this time were very different from intimations of God and immortality. I swung to the other extreme and in bitterness I said: "There is no God." As I see it now, there was more real religion in that cry of despair than in the years of complacency and second-hand Christianity.

How, then, did I obtain bread?

By the dreadful expedient of selling my library. Charing Cross Road became my Via Dolorosa. I became painfully familiar with Foyles, for it did not take me long to find out that the Foyle brothers would buy almost anything, compared with other secondhand bookshops, all of which were rather selective, altogether finicky, I thought. The bookseller would take a book into his hand, casually turn over the pages, then hand it back with the remark—"That's no good to me." It was with a sick heart that I made my way out. The prices offered were calamitous, but, at least, Foyles did buy: blessed be their name! I could be sure of walking out of their shop with the next week's rent and a few shillings for food, which was a great thing.

It is a temptation to linger over that library which I had to exchange for bread, though I cannot describe the pain its disposal brought me. It enshrined years of struggle and sacrifice, aspiration and zest, avidly-acquired knowledge and ideas. I shed tears of misery and pain, as I made up a parcel of books for sale. It was no specialist's or scholar's library but wide ranging, its basis a number of standard encyclopaedias, a large range of works by leading historians, philosophers and Fathers of the Church, commentaries, texts, biographies, English standard literature and contemporary writers. My Russian shelves I was especially proud of. I was well-off in economics—Adam Smith, Ricardo, Mill, Marshall, Taussig, Marx. I had a varied lot of odds and ends in science, art, music and ceramics. In the course of a terrible year, all these books went in the task of keeping soul and body together. At the end there remained only a few hundred, which not even Foyles would purchase; these were taken by an antique furniture dealer in Palmer's Green for five shillings.

To live through all this meant that I ceased to struggle, which played havoc with my sense of responsibility. Work of any kind was unobtainable. It would have been easier for me to obtain a peerage. So I gave up caring. I drifted as long as I had books to dispose of. What was to happen after that I refused to contemplate.

Religion had ceased to count at all. I never went near a church. Sundays and weekdays were alike, except that on Sundays I could not visit the British Museum Reading Room, where I spent most of my days. I read nothing but books dealing with music. It was a curious experience. I felt a deep fellow-feeling for Schubert and Mozart. I read voraciously the stories of Wagner, Tchaikovsky and Moussorgsky, but Beethoven was the pole-star.

One remains oneself, I suppose, even in the deepest ditch. I took an Evening Institute course on the development of musical forms and orchestration, which proved to be useful later on. But at the time I had no utilitarian object in mind whatsoever. To take this course meant going without food, for the few miserable shillings I got for my books did not run to anything but food. Any other expenditure meant so much less to eat. I must indeed have been hungry for musical knowledge.

2

I was approaching the end of my tether.

During this time, I kept away from all my friends. I particularly steered clear of all ministerial contacts. Years later, when I told a little of this story to Dr. Berry, when he was secretary of the Congregational Union, he said: "Why didn't you come to see me?" The fact is that failure and poverty had bred a desolating bitterness in my heart. In the darkness of such bitterness, I saw the churches as nothing but organized hypocrisy and avoided them. On Sundays I started the habit of attending the so-called ethical churches, and discovered what was even more attractive—the Sunday evening Chamber Music concerts at the Conway Hall in Red Lion Square. Music was my one great consolation. It was escape from my misery.

My wife, who was in Southport during all this time, dependent on her family, urged me to visit old friends of hers in Enfield, the Lewis Phillips. At last I went. Never can I be sufficiently grateful for their utter kindness and Christian care. I told them the truth about my condition. Without hesitation, they pressed me to come and stay with them: a great act of mercy on their part. Lewis Phillips was carrying a heavy load; an ailing wife, Beckie—one of the most beautiful spirits it has been my blessing to meet; three children at the most expensive period of their rearing; and an aged father. But he insisted on adding me to the family. Not only that, he insisted that Edith must also come. "You two," he said, "have been separated long enough." And for three months, he took us in. Not once, by word or deed, did they make us feel not wanted. They were those rarest of human beings—genuine Christians.

While in Enfield I landed a job. In sober fact it was the occupation of addressing envelopes, from 9 a.m. to 6 p.m., with an hour off for lunch. It seemed marvellous when I was told to start work. After a year of painful unemployment and wretched penury, it was paradise to be earning an income of my own once again. My interest in men and the world was reborn, and everything began to wear a brighter hue. My wife found a top-floor flat in Palmer's Green, only a two-roomed flat and very small compared with the nine-roomed manse we had occupied in Southport. But it was our own.

And she joined me at the job of envelope-addressing. After a month we were able to get the furniture and household effects from Southport to London. And so we became London citizens.

There may be worse jobs than addressing envelopes for eight hours a day in a basement, on behalf of the distribution of Force and Sunny Jim, but I should want convincing on the point. The conditions of the office in which we worked were comparatively good; the employers were most considerate and treated their employees well; but the archangel Gabriel could not have divested envelope-addressing of its soul-destroying character, so utterly mechanical, requiring no intelligence or initiative whatever. Work that an idiot, not too far gone, could have performed. By six o'clock I had no vitality left, far too tired to do any serious reading, all I wanted was to sleep. From one prison I had landed into another.

The consciousness of this became more and more galling as time went on, but I had a horror of returning to the poverty and insecurity from which the job had rescued us. Fits of depression were of increasing recurrence. Now and again, I used to get scared and panic-stricken. The future held no prospect. I was "too old at forty"—and had visions of being driven from pillar to post. But in between the moods, I gritted my teeth and determined somehow, though how I had no idea, that I would get out of it and find myself a career.

Music was my only interest—and there was no career in that, for I was merely a listener. I spent a few shillings each week in buying gramophone records, and was accumulating a library of records. Most evenings found me at home listening to the symphonies and pianoforte concertos of Beethoven. Philosophy, theology, politics had passed out of my life. For the greater part of the day, I was a machine (an inefficient one), but for a few hours each night a human being.

Providence came to my aid in bringing the work to an end. The thing I dreaded most came to pass. There had been rumours for weeks that the job was finishing, but as each week went by and the sword did not fall, I thought it would go on and on. At last we were informed that our services would no longer be required.

That Friday evening I felt reckless. I cocked a snook at Fate. Instead of going home with Edith to Palmer's Green, I went to Soho and got a good dinner, with a bottle of wine. I felt like the little mouse which ran into a beer-barrel to escape the attentions of the cat; after a bellyful of beer, it staggered up to the rim of the barrel and shouted: "Where's that damned cat?" But the effect, alas, soon passed. I turned into one of the little cafés in Compton Street and got into conversation with a variety of odd fish. Finally I found myself in Coventry Street and decided to have a coffee at Lyons' Corner House.

I sat at a table alone. I had a copy of Romain Rolland's *Beethoven the Creator*, which I placed on the table. After a while a man sat at my table. I could see him eyeing the book. "Excuse me," he said at last, "but are you particularly interested in Beethoven?" That question started a conversation in which I did most of the talking. Here was a discussion between two human beings about something that mattered. "You have read Thayer?" he asked in tones of incredulity. The upshot was that my casual companion asked for my address. "A most interesting talk," he said as he wished me good night.

A few days later I received a letter from His Master's Voice, Oxford St., asking if I would go to see Mr. Kerridge. There I found my acquaintance of the Corner House. He wanted to know if I was prepared to do lecturing on music. He wanted someone who would lecture to ordinary, musically uncultivated people on the appreciation of good music, nothing technical was required. "If you can talk in public about music as well as you talked to me the other night," he said, "you are the man I want." I assured him I could talk better in public than in private, which was not untrue! And though I had never lectured on music, I had an amateur's enthusiasm and a fair knowledge of the things likely to interest an audience. So I was engaged to lecture to gramophone societies, church literary fellowships, schools and other organizations on the appreciation of music, illustrating my talks with gramophone records. So my reading during those months of misery was to come in useful after all.

With that stroke of luck my temperament began to rise again. To lecture on music—and be paid for it! I reflected that had I gone home the previous Friday, and not drunk that bottle of Sauterne, I should not have met Mr. Kerridge, and should have missed this opportunity!

The job was too good to last long, but it was enjoyable, apart from occasional bursts of inner dissatisfaction. Now and again, after one of my lectures, I would be seized with a sudden sense of the futility of what I was doing. I remembered that all my life I had been fighting for ideas and causes; but here I was paddling in a backstream, talking about musicians dead and gone to a lot of comfortable easygoing people. I became overborne by nostalgia for the battlefield. But these moods did not last, and I enjoyed my dalliance.

I did not become a member of the staff of H.M.V. I was no more than a free-lance lecturer, with this difference, that I was busily occupied; and the company, through local dealers, supplied machines and records for purposes of demonstration. My remuneration was comparatively good, and I was comfortably placed. What was also of importance was that I became in a position to acquire records cheaply, and my friend put a good deal of record-reviewing in my way. So I gradually built up an extensive library of records which I still possess.

I lectured a good deal to young people's societies in

churches, usually with the minister in the chair, and I flatter myself that I generally succeeded in interesting those audiences in particular.

This was a dilettante kind of existence. I looked for all the free concerts and the cheap ones. Saturday afternoons found me either at the Chamber Music concerts at the Victoria and Albert Museum or at St. Martin-in-the-Fields, Sunday afternoons at the Palladium Orchestral Concerts, and Sunday evenings either at Morley College or Conway Hall. This I varied with visits to the museums, especially the Science and Natural History Museum in Kensington. My spirit was hibernating. I was passing through a form of convalescence after the battering of that first year in London.

At Conway Hall, one Sunday morning, I made friends with Kilburn Scott, a Yorkshire engineer. He was a real character, a dabbler in all sorts of things, and especially keen on the out-of-the-way movements in which London abounds. One Sunday morning after "service", he wanted to know what I was doing the following evening. He wanted me to accompany him to a meeting at 55 Gower Street, in Bloomsbury. When I asked what the meeting was about he was rather vague. "There's a fellow there," he said, "a foreigner of some sort, preaching a new religion." That did not appeal to me at all, for I had finished with religions, old and new. I said, No. Scott, however, was very insistent. "You come along," he urged, "you've never heard a man talk like yon chap, nor seen one like him either." So I consented, to please him, and on the following Monday evening we entered a packed drawing-room at Gower Street. It proved to be the most extraordinary meeting I had ever attended in my life. It shattered "the even tenour of my ways". It flung me into a maelstrom compared to which my past conflicts were as a gentle shower to a tornado.

A silver-haired lady was addressing the meeting. Her face fascinated me more than her words, for it had the stamp of distinction, indeed of uniqueness. But I made nothing of what she was saying. It was something about the need of a new nation and a new Europe. The words "New Britain" were repeated, like a recurring decimal, a queer jumble of ideas: economics and the stomach, politics and the heart, culture and the head. I gave up trying to follow. After she sat down, the chairman threw the meeting open to discussion, and a variety of people expressed their mainly trite opinions. Then a man got up at the back of the room, a huge figure of a man, with a dominating head. He spoke for about twenty minutes. What he said gripped me. I felt something fall away from me. I cannot recall now the theme of his speech, but I had never heard English like it. Its grammar was English, but that was all. He endowed words with meaning that held my heart like a vice. I recall him saying that the human will was not the will to exist, to survive, that was animal; man was spirit, dominated by the will to glory, to power, to ecstasy. It sounded marvellous to me.

I was so tremendously moved and excited, painfully so, that I got on my feet and let myself go. I have forgotten what I said, even if I knew at the time. Some deep, suppressed hunger and awareness welled up in my heart and tore through my words: now I was alive again.

My speech made an impression. Indeed, "impression" was too weak a word. It swept that meeting into enthusiasm, and people crowded around to congratulate me. I was in a whirl. Then the speaker of the evening, the lady of silver beauty, whispered to me: "Will you please come downstairs, Mr. Mitrinović would like to meet you." With a heart beating like a battering ram, I followed her into the basement. On what adventure was I embarking? Down, down— it seemed endless—until I was ushered into a book-lined room. There before the fireplace stood the big man. He smiled and greeted me with the dramatic words: "Come on. You are the man I've been seeking for the last fourteen years!"

This Mitrinović merits at least one whole book to himself. Let me say that he immediately swept me into slavish devotion. He asked me to give up music lecturing and throw in my lot with him, to help him in the task "of planning a new European revolution of order and spirit". I did not hesitate for a second. Never were bridges burnt with such fierce gaiety or passionate ardour. That night the old life was dead. A new one had started.

3

Let me indicate here, before I go further, what I regard as the significance of my first few years in London, and anticipate somewhat. When I arrived in London, my faith in social progress was unimpaired, for it had become my religion. The point I want to make is that my heart had become completely divorced from the church, which, I felt, was one of the strongholds of the existing order and an enemy to true progress, which I thought of entirely in terms of Socialism. Despite my bitterness with the local Labour movement in Southport, I was certainly looking forward to working in the London Socialist movement as soon as I had solved the economic problem of daily bread; but the severity of that struggle knocked the party stuffing out of me, and in the course of my first year in London Socialism ceased to count in my life. I was stranded. The Church had vanished and its substitute had also disappeared. In my second year, music as a merely individual means of enjoyment had absorbed me to the exclusion of all else.

That I had fitful stirrings of revolt against this condition of things offered evidence that I was not satisfied. So when I met Mitrinović, the suppressed need for social significance, for a faith to live by, broke out unhindered. My striving for social change and individual fulfilment had become comprehended entirely within a human, secular, this-worldly framework. Even Christianity of the idealized, non-institutional kind, had then ceased to be decisive in my thinking. Christianity, along with science, music and socialism, was one of the products of the European mind. It was human effort and co-operation and organization that alone mattered.

CHAPTER VIII

RENAISSANCE

THE FIRST STEP in my association with Mitrinović was to leave Palmer's Green, though my wife continued to live there. He said it was necessary for me to live near him, so I was given rooms in Fitzroy Street. I used to visit Palmer's Green on Sundays for the day, but before long, my wife found a flat in Oakley Square, where we did not stay long. Then we moved to Westbourne Square, where we had quite a commodious apartment. But shortly after we settled there, Edith was taken ill and had to go to hospital. She never really recovered, and in March, 1934, she died.

In the meantime I lived in a whirl of meetings, public and private, from luncheon till early dawn. I felt how wonderful it was! I was given plenty of money, though I had little occasion to spend it for I was lavishly entertained. The Age of Plenty had dawned. It did not last, of course. As long as it continued I became familiar with expensive restaurants and no longer trembled before a head waiter. This was revolutionary conspiracy in a new style. Unlike the revolutionists who had prepared the great upheavals of the past, I lived in abundance. Mitrinović was a man of amazing generosity. He had no sense of *meum* and *teum*. For property and money (its symbol) he had utter contempt. I once saw him throw a bundle of pound notes into the air before an astonished company of people. He looked on with sardonic amusement at the scramble. He had an unerring eye for the weakness of people. I could relate endless stories of his generosity. Let me tell this one.

I was lecturing at Oxford to a school of foreign students on the politics of this New European movement, when in walked Mitrinović. When the meeting was over, I asked

118

him what he was doing in Oxford. "I came to hear your lecture," he replied, which was nonsense. "Go and get your bag from your hotel, wherever it is and come with me." He took me to the Randolph Hotel and entertained me as though I were royalty. The following morning, he put his hand in his waistcoat pocket (a very famous pocket) and gave me a five-pound note. "For liberty," he said, as he bade me good-bye.

There were meetings inspired by him at Gower Street and elsewhere all day and night, and every day and night. I was getting acquainted with all sorts of people, famous and obscure. Gone were the apathy and depression of the recent past. Once again I walked with my head high. My anonymity vanished. I had the grand feeling that I had my hands on the levers of history. Was I not helping to initiate a new order of civilization for Britain and Europe?

I

Let me try to give briefly a connected idea of what Mitrinović was aiming at. He was Serbian by birth, but the basic fact was that he was "a good European", and his dearest political object was to create a United Europe. He talked European Federation when many of the people clamouring for it to-day sneered at the idea and at him. But the European Federation he was advocating was very different from the ideas being discussed now. To him Europe was fundamentally a community of persons, of which states, parliaments, industry and all other institutions were mere functions.

The significance of Europe to him lay in the fact that it was the home and ground of individual self-consciousness. It was in Europe that the human species had emerged into individual personality, by virtue of which it exercised leadership of the world. The problem Mitrinović was trying to solve was this: How to enable individual self-consciousness to develop. He saw the real crisis of the modern world to lie in the continued existence of the person; he thought self-consciousness to be imperilled. The symbol of this danger was the mass-man: what he called the Block-State. It was the danger that became so dramatically obvious in Nazism. It was the danger, too, which was the theme of those other good Europeans, Unamuno, Ortega y Gasset and Jaspers.

Now, the solution of the problem necessitated a complete and revolutionary transformation of the entire European Order, but a revolution that must be voluntary, conscious and planned. It must, in short, be a revolution of order. A revolution for the purpose of preserving self-consciousness would defeat its own end if it were effected by necessity, by the mere dialectical operation of unconscious forces. Hence his opposition to class-war and the Marxian idea. Hence his opposition also to acquiesence in a conflict of two opposite forces—Capitalism against Socialism, Fascism versus Communism. The dialectics of such conflict would place the trump card in the hands of necessity. There is, he used to declare, another force, a Third Force, above and between the opposites, the force of self-conscious persons, acting together as a voluntary unity. Only such a "force" could save self-consciousness.

To guarantee the existence of persons, power must, he declared, be decentralized. There must be a devolutionary process throughout society. The Block-State had to be broken up, Europe reduced to regions, the nations to small communities in organic relation to one another. It was a great idea, the re-creation of the Greek City-States, with this difference—that the whole of Europe was to become one community of inter-related city-states. Let the communities govern themselves in all matters which exclusively concerned them. Matters affecting only a region to be decided only by that region; matters affecting a number of regions, such as a province or a country, to be decided by the province or country; matters affecting the communities as a whole to be decided by them all. Devolve power so that small communities can act autonomously; then federate them in a grand confederation to enable them to act as a unity in those things concerning them all. Devolution and Federation—those were Mitrinović's key-words.

Now, he went on, the moment you begin devolution, you discover that in every community some things concern everybody, others concern only some. So there must be a separation of powers within the community as well as decentralization. Food and material needs affect everybody; laws may be general, they may also concern only particular communities, for other areas demand different laws. So, said he, separate economics from politics. Let there be one body or authority for economics, another for politics, another for culture. That was something like the idea of the Three-Fold State, the subject of one of Rudolf Steiner's books. The three authorities in each community and country and in the community as a whole would be co-ordinated in a fourth body, the Senate. This corresponds to the structure and function of the human body, said Mitrinović: stomach, economics; heart, politics; the head, culture; the fourth body, the senate, the glandular system.

To bring this about there must be a transformation of industrial ownership and structure, which has been made technically possible by the development of production and finance. There is no need for revolutionary violence and expropriation. By the nationalization of finance, it will be possible to compensate the present owners who will yield up their power. So ultimately there would be integration of economic authority in the whole of Europe.

The revolution of order must, he contended, begin in Great Britain because of her position as a colonizing world-power, and her historic task of mediating European civilization to the world. That was why, said Mitrinović, he had come to England to live and work. He had landed in London at the outbreak of the first world-war in August, 1914, and the first thing which he, a Serb, encountered when he got off the train at Victoria was a *John Bull* poster—then under the editorship of Horatio Bottomley—"To hell with the Serbs!" His mission was to persuade sufficient British people to bring about this revolution of spirit and order, to create a New Britain. The fruit of New Britain, would be New France, New Spain, New Germany, and ultimately New Europe.

How to get hold of people sufficiently awakened and sensitive to respond to this vision, was his problem. A difficult problem, certainly. So Mitrinović held semi-public meetings at No. 55, Gower St., and from the audiences he combed out selected individuals. These individuals he then proceeded to weld together into a conscious unity. This process I did not discover until later. It proceeded by stages, the last of which was rather a gruesome business, a species of psychological "third-degree". He had to be fairly sure of a man or woman before attempting it. The first stage was oil and honey, which was the one I was in. It comprised very subtle flattery, of which Mitrinović was the complete master. When I had passed to the veteran stage, I used to watch him at work on others. It was a wonderful performance, from which I derived sensuous pleasure and satisfaction. Almost all fell for it like ripe plums in late summer. Everybody submitted to his uncanny power to charm. I saw some very prominent people captive to him, among them the Dean of Canterbury and Aneurin Bevan. I recall only one whom Mitrinović failed to impress, the communist, John Lewis, one-time national organizer of the Left-Book Club.

Mitrinović was a marvellous talker, but a still more marvellous listener. That is how he first approached a prospective disciple: he encouraged him to talk, and listened with intense concentration. Suddenly he would break forth excitedly and turning to the company present would say: "Did you hear that? You should have been taking notes.

Absolutely wonderful!" It is likely that the man had been talking utter platitudes. I shall not forget the effect upon myself. I swelled visibly. I was completely taken in. Mitrinović listened open-mouthed to me and on occasion took notes himself. I began to think I was a truly apocalyptic man.

He discovered what the particular individual considered to be his own strong point, and fastened upon it. He soon found out that I was inordinately proud of my oratorical gifts. So he exploited my vanity. When the time for flattery was passed, he used the same vanity to humiliate me. He then referred to me, smilingly, as the Prima Donna. But not at first. He was not so crude as to pile on verbal flattery. He did it by deeds. In a meeting he would pass a note to me after someone had made a criticism or asked a question to state: "You deal with this point; the answer to it needs a trained speaker." He could inveigle a rabbit out of its hole.

In all this, he was faithfully supported by a very devoted band of followers, mostly women (some brilliant and powerful). They followed his cue without hesitation. They would take notes of my speeches and conversations, ask me questions and write down the answer, get up in a meeting after I had spoken, to point out to the meeting the "tremendous" importance of the speech I had just made, and so on. Sometimes it was rather clumsily done. And then "The Old Man" intervened. Woe betide the bungler!

By these and other methods Mitrinović held me firmly by a strong leash. I was prepared to do anything for him. But he subtly refrained from asking me to do what he knew I would not like to do. That was a basic part of the technique. He did not strain one's loyalty to begin with.

A new movement had just been initiated by him called "The Eleventh Hour for the advocacy of Social Credit and the paying of a national dividend to every citizen". I was made "National Organizer". Colonel James Delahaye was the "Chancellor", an office whose exact function I never understood. I took the whole thing very seriously, and set about the work with a will. Public meetings were held every Monday evening. I interviewed many people. One of my first victims was the Marquess of Tavistock, afterwards Duke of Bedford, who ran a little movement of his own with something of the same objects. We amalgamated and printed subscription forms and leaflets and did a multitude of things; but no results followed, and before long the joint movement died very quietly. Mitrinović did not intend any results. The meetings served his purpose by giving him contacts with persons who might prove to be useful for his major aims.

Lest I be misunderstood, let me make it clear that Mitrinović was completely sincere, objective and personally disinterested. He deliberately flattered and exploited the weakness of people so as to win them for the ideas he was interested in. And whatever may be said of his methods, his objectives and ideas were magnificent. I cannot imagine anyone more utterly devoted to his task than he. Night and day he worked to promote it in his own way, on which he insisted. His whole being was identified with the cause he had at heart. He was the slave of the idea and insisted on your being its slave too. He was absorbed in great ends. There was nothing in the least provincial or parochial about him. He moved among the stars. He could truly repeat John Wesley's great affirmation—"The world is my parish".

The Eleventh Hour Movement which ran its brief course was, however, but a curtain-raiser to the much more ambitious attempt to launch the New Britain Movement, which came about in 1933. It was in connection with this that I started my journalistic career as an editor!

2

Mitrinović was firmly determined to get not only a paper but a Press. In his more expansive moments, he talked about seven daily papers circulating throughout Europe in different languages. The first thing, however, was a London weekly.

Late one Sunday night in August, 1932, after a day in Bournemouth, I was at supper in Bogey's bar, in Southampton Row. There I found Mitrinović—an unexpected and pleasurable meeting. He broke the news to me that he was bringing out *The New Britain Quarterly*, in October, "and you are to be the editor", he said casually. The fact that I knew nothing about the trade of journalism or of type setting, lay-out and a hundred and one other things was immaterial. That I was to edit was the great thing: I was immediately in ecstasy. I took my new appointment seriously. This was much better than being "National Organizer". I burst with a sense of importance, and set about the task of planning the first number. But Mitrinović could not be got to discuss it with me. Time after time he brushed aside the suggestions I made. He wanted to talk about something else. But at last he asked me to go to the printers and discuss the size, format and other details of the proposed quarterly. I did so, and got a dummy copy made up in a green cover, similar in size and shape to the *XXth Century* magazine. I was very excited and proud, proud as Lucifer. When I took this outcome of hours of work with the printer to Mitrinović, he threw it into the waste-paper basket after one withering, contemptuous look. "You are not going to stab the Unconscious of the Englishman with *that* kind of thing," he said. And in the next ten minutes he sketched out the format and design of the magazine. "Take that to the printer," he said. It was a most extraordinary size, 16″ by 14″, with a three-column page. I was dismayed. The printer was provoked to ribald laughter. But that was to be its format. I began to learn that to be editor meant being Mitrinović's office-boy. It was the first rift in the lute.

A few weeks' later, a newcomer to the group, Watson Thompson, was made co-editor with me. I didn't like that at all—usurping a place on my fine throne. Mitrinović made the same fuss of him as he had made of me; but Thompson was a good fellow and we became good friends. He was the most clerical layman I had ever met. His every utterance was a sermon. He sweated a peculiar kind of secular piety. Yet we had a long partnership and went through the mill together. We were Mitrinović's "See-saw, Marjorie Daw", as he said himself. When I was in favour, Thompson was out of it, and vice-versa. So we developed a deep fellow-feeling. He was an efficient worker and a really capable organizer, and displaced me as the Boss's office boy on the *Quarterly*, which gave me freedom to do what I liked—book-reviewing and article writing. That, at least, was a sub-stantial gain, for the *Quarterly* helped me to serve an apprenticeship as a writer. It also brought me into contact with interesting, distinguished people—and cranks.

Of the distinguished ones, I would put first, Professor Frederick Soddy, lately Lee Professor of Chemistry at Oxford. He had developed a monetary theory of his own in *Wealth, Virtual Wealth and Debt*. The New Britain Movement committed itself to his monetary doctrine, which was based on the assumption that the banks had usurped the people's right (vested in the King) to create money. He was a very imperious man with an undisguised contempt for those who differed from him, and never suffered fools gladly. He was a porcupine: he bristled, and when he bristled, he was sharp. His favourite weapon, however, was the sledge-hammer, for he had no idea of how to handle a rapier. In a crowded meeting at Edinburgh, he asked the question—"What is Money?" One member of the audience was foolish enough to answer. "Rubbish," said Soddy, "that gentleman has got his answer from the books. He doesn't know anything about it. I'll tell him." I often had to pour oil on troubled waters after he had spoken at meetings. But I had great respect and affection for him. To me he was always kind, if blunt. On one occasion he summarily told Mitrinović that "Davies knows nothing of monetary theory". Six months later when I took the chair for him at Glastonbury, I had the satisfac-tion of hearing him say, in the introduction to his lecture, that I was one of the few who really understood his arguments. In the intervening six months I had been busy on the study of his theory.

Another friend of that period was Professor John Macmurray, of University College, London, for whom I have nothing but the greatest regard, and his jolly, unaffected wife. Macmurray can be intellectually perverse, as only a professor can. His fatal weakness is intellectualism, which incapacitates him as an interpreter of Christianity. I found him familiar with the Bible as literature, but a stranger to its ethos, its world, its essential meaning. Which is paradoxical, for the idea of man as person is central in Macmurray's philosophy.

At this time I also came to know S. G. Hobson, whom Mintrinović wanted to write for his *Quarterly*. When he knew of this friendship, Montague Fordham said to me: "So you've got Sam Hobson writing for you. If Sam were one of the Twelve Apostles, he would find a reason for resigning in less than a month!" If Soddy was a porcupine, Hobson was a hedgehog. He was all toes, with corns on every one of them. But I grew very fond of him. He had done notable work on Guild Socialism in the pages of the old *New Age* under the brilliant A. R. Orage, and had been a well-known Fabian: Mitrinović held him up as one of the founding fathers of his new movement. Poor Hobson had fallen on evil days, but Mitrinović picked him up, and it was interesting to see how gradually he mellowed towards the end.

Orage was one of the idols of my Manchester youth, so it was a great thrill when Mitrinović got me to meet him. He was long past his best, however, then, but even so, he was easily the pick of the Douglas Social Credit group, many of whom I came to know fairly intimately, from Douglas himself downward. In his *New English Weekly*, Orage tried to make an impossible come-back, for he thought he could do anything. He gave me the feeling of a profoundly disillusioned man. He had spent years with that strange man,

Gurdjieff, and underwent terrible physical and mental discipline. He said to me a few nights before his sudden death, after broadcasting, that after the age of fifty the soul knew it was stranded. When the *Quarterly* appeared I believe the first number sold about 2,000 copies. Mitrinović had been right, for its odd format made an immediate appeal. I got great satisfaction from the sight of my name as its co-editor, and from the initials D. D. at the foot of the reviews. For some reason, Mitrinović was against the use of my middle name, Richard.

The second number was not a success and proved to be the last, though a third number appeared under the title *Atlantic Alliance*, in which Mitrinović wrote an "open letter to Hitler", calling him "saint" and "selfless being" appealing to him to start the European Federation! This symbolized Mitrinović's fatal and fundamental weakness: his adherence to fantasy. Yet he combined with this a profound skill in political analysis, which would not stop him making bizarre and utterly impossible proposals. I sometimes wondered whether he was not pulling all our legs. It was this apparent lack of realism that seemed to prevent him from realizing the disastrous effect of giving successive numbers of a magazine a new title. A fourth number of the *Quarterly* came out as *New Albion*.

Long before this, however, I was in revolt, and indulged in what Mitrinović called an "outing". I could not stand his whirl and racket. Behind the outer helter-skelter, which, God knows, was enough to exhaust a rhinoceros, there went an inner process of psycho-analytic "skinning", which will form the subject of the next chapter, an experience which was enough to shatter a dinosaur. After a few weeks of retreat, Thompson would be sent to look me up with a "special message". Back I would go, to be treated as the prodigal son in the parable. They killed the fatted calf to the accompaniment of music and merry making. These "outings" were an established practice for members of Mitrinović's inner circle, with very few exceptions. There was never a time when someone or other was not having one of his or her absences. Some never came back. The occasion was to come when I, too, was never to return. But my association with Mitrinović went on for seven years: I severed it, though not my friendship for him, in 1938.

During these seven years, I read a great deal, though the opportunity was hard to come by because of the eternal round of meetings, group gatherings and talk. My by no means infrequent "outings" gave me at least the opportunity for reading. Long, calm days, blessedly free from interruptions. As was my habit, I got through a great deal. This reading was now confined almost entirely to economics and psychology, though occasionally I had spells of political study. I made a close examination of monetary theory, both orthodox and heterodox, and got down to an examination of Douglas' Social Credit and the precious A + B theorem, which I came to the conclusion to be nothing but confused nonsense. It is remarkable how many distinguished Anglican clergy have been hypnotized by it, but that is by the way. In addition to Soddy, I waded through Gesell's *Natural Economic Order* and Buchi's exposition of it. Gesell was a sturdy radical and betrayed a hopeless incapacity to understand capitalism and the idea of dynamic historic development. He aimed at trying to restore the primitive capitalism of the eighteenth century. Very different was the work of Keynes, Cole, Robertson, Von Hayek, Robbins and Von Mises. But the major element in my reading during this period was technocratic literature, mostly American. I saturated myself with the statistics of modern productive capacity. Not only did I read Stuart Chase, Loeb and Geddings, but I kept an eye on technical journals as well. I got to the point of being able to reel off figures by the yard, which used to impress audiences.

I also did a great deal of reading in Guild Socialism, the earlier works of G. D. H. Cole, the work of Hobson, Orage,

Carpenter, Penty—which led me to the French Syndicalists, and to Sorel. From them I tackled Proudhon's *What is Property?*, and the Anarchists, Reclus, Kropotkin, Emma Goldman. There was a certain amount of re-reading for I had been familiar with Syndicalism in my trade-union days. My position in Mitrinović's movement imposed this study upon me, and indeed he actively encouraged it, giving me much guidance, for in fact he had mastered the subject.

Another field of reading was psychology, or rather psychopathology. The circle round Mitrinović contained many psychoanalysts, amateur and professional. I had been told to get equipped to understand the language they spoke. Not only did I read Adler in particular, I lived psycho-analysis. Mitrinović knew it all thoroughly. At his suggestion I even underwent a long course of psycho-analysis. In fact, I lent myself to more than one amateur analyst of the circle, and came to be on intimate terms with my Unconscious, and not even Dr. Groddeck's assertions about the Id, the Unc as we called it, could frighten me.

Mitrinović himself asserted that I suffered from birth trauma, from a difficult parturition. He said I was reluctant to leave the comfort of the womb. How did he know? Among the many psychologists I met was Dr. Künkel of Berlin, author of *How to be Normal.* In a lecture to our group, his psychology seemed to me a thinly-veiled justification for Nazism. I did not hesitate to say so. Künkel was typical of the accommodative cowardice of the German professional class. He built up a very fanciful structure, leading to the conclusion that Germany was on the way to normality, to the transcending of the twentieth-century neurosis. I told Dr. Künkel that only a neurotic people could possibly tolerate Hitler.

3

I recovered my enthusiasm for Mitrinović with the launching of the New Britain movement and its weekly organ,

New Britain, the first number of which appeared on Empire Day, 1933. It was a great success. But the history of the movement as well as of the paper was one long procession of missed opportunities. I am convinced that in the idea and essence of this movement there was the antidote to both Fascism and Communism. Paradoxical as it may seem, in the seething brains of a Serbian philosopher there was conceived a programme that supremely expressed the genius and character of the British nation and peoples. "You can do nothing in England," Mitrinović used to say, "unless you unite the Bible and the Union Jack. Even their football crowds sing 'Abide with Me'." What the world interpreted as British hypocrisy, he believed to contain the historic mission of the British race. It was intuitive genius.

Through the incredible sacrifices of a few individuals who ventured their all, the weekly, *New Britain*, was launched on its career. Seventy thousand copies were printed of the first number, and its net sales for the first three months were amazing. Its editor, C. B. Purdom, had been responsible for *Everyman*, the literary weekly owned by the publishers, J. M. Dent and Sons, until they sold it the year before, when Mitrinović set out to get hold of its editor for his own long desired weekly.

Under circumstances of the greatest difficulty, C. B. succeeded in producing a first-rate weekly. It was advertised as "A sixpenny Weekly for 2d.", and the claim was absolutely true. Purdom got together a fine group of regular contributors, including Major General Fuller, Hugh Quigley, Matthew Norgate, Frederick Soddy, John Grierson, and a great many well-known names. The paper was admirably made up, printed on a greenish paper, something like the old *Westminster Gazette*, a first-class production in every way. But Purdom was an experienced and independent editor, and Mitrinović was unable to play with him as he had with others; in particular he refused to allow one of Mitrinović's intimate women followers to have her name on the paper as co-editor. She had no journalistic knowledge, and he did not intend to provide the opportunity for any interference. The most he would agree to was to give her the nominal position of assistant editor, and undertook to train her in the work; so far as I know she never took advantage of the offer. Certainly the weekly was a lively and attractive paper, outspoken, sensible, maintaining a proper balance between politics and the arts. Mitrinović himself, under the pseudonym of Cosmoi, contributed a series of profound articles on "World Affairs". Readers complained that they couldn't understand them. Their English certainly was most bizarre and outlandish. With a touch of mischief, C. B. advised readers to read them *four times*. Mitrinović was saying something new, he said. And like all pioneering geniuses, he had to create a clientèle that would understand him. In the last century, critics said the same things about Browning, that he was abstruse, obscure, nonsensical. Tennyson they understood: he fetched the handkerchiefs out of their pockets with the greatest ease; but Browning had to wait. Mitrinović, too, has to wait. A profounder thinker than Browning, he will probably have to wait longer. No wonder that those earnest readers of *New Britain* could not understand him, though they read his article forty times.

With the publication of the paper, the Movement was started. It was a most stirring time. The office was entirely separate from that of the newspaper, and we were literally snowed under with applications for speakers. Groups were started all over the country. In London they sprang up like mushrooms. I was once more made National Organizer. For the second time I felt I was making history.

If there was one man who should not have been appointed a national organizer, that was myself. I was unfit to organize a Sunday School treat, let alone a national movement. Such a confession does not imply any humility on my part, for organizing is most definitely not one of my gifts. But had I been a really capable organizer I should not have been able to organize this New Britain Movement. Since I am trying to tell the truth I must state that, to the best of my belief, Mitrinović did not intend the movement to be organized, most certainly not as a popular party. Even as late as August, 1934, just before the second national conference at Glastonbury, he did not seem to have made up his mind whether New Britain was to be a political movement or a spiritual fraternity. After a year and a half of chaotic, frustrated attempts at political organization, I was flabbergasted at Mitrinović's uncertainty, which he communicated to me during a taxi-ride to a meeting. It was this confusion that was the source of the chaos and conflict behind the movement. And what a chaos! As one of its secretaries put it, New Britain was a bottomless abyss into which documents, plans and programmes disappeared for ever and ever. That the movement grew to the dimensions it did, in spite of chaos and unbelievable incompetence, was a testimony to the spiritual vitality of its vision.

These two conceptions of New Britain—that of an active political party and that of a spiritual aristocracy—were locked in an internecine conflict. C. B. Purdom at first was the protagonist of the political idea, looking upon the affair as a practical man. He said we must get down to brass tacks and organize, and he did his mortal best. He started a million shilling fund. He gathered round him a collection of big business executives and professional people. At Mitrinović's suggestion he even included British Israelites, with whom he seemed to get on very well. The leaders of all the London and provincial groups, except Rugby, Liverpool and Oxford, rallied round Purdom. But behind the scenes, Mitrinović, through his close adherents, of whom I was for the moment one, reduced these attempts to nullity. On the inside, he made the feathers fly, though outside, the movement continued to grow rapidly. I was engaged nearly every night addressing meetings from Bristol in the West to Glasgow and Edinburgh in the North. The groups multiplied and were a live force. A great public meeting was organized at the Caxton Hall when there was an overflowing audience. Purdom was in the chair, as he was on nearly all other important public occasions thereafter, for Mitrinović valued his skill in the chair and his ability to control not only the meeting but the platform. There appeared to be a full tide of success.

What was the programme of the Movement? Purdom printed one in the paper week by week: National Dividends, devolution of Parliament, Workers' Control in Industry, Atlantic Alliance (i.e. alliance between the British Empire and the United States of America), European Federation. What gave the movement drive and vitality was a spiritual, personal idea which came to be known as P.A., Personal Alliance. This was a pledge, or agreement, which members of the groups made to preserve and promote their interests as universal, personal, human beings. The political proposals derived their force from P.A. They were conceived so as to facilitate personal relationships. The idea was that to make such personal relations universally possible, such and such political changes must be effected. The real crisis of the modern world was the peril to personality. Therefore, above all things, preserve the person. That was the message.

This, I am convinced, is profoundly true. It is the reality behind the struggle everywhere for political freedom. Shall *persons* exist? In a society that was suppressing personal identity under mass anonymity, destroying the sense of validity and worthwhileness in common people, P.A. acted with dynamic force. Its effect was to make people feel that they were somebody. And so New Britain grew at a fabulous pace. It was the answer to Fascism. And to Communism also. Fascism gave validity through enslavement, so does Communism. New Britain was an attempt to give validity through freedom and equality, by personal alliance. Young people joined in great numbers, because, I am convinced, it enabled them to feel they were capable of mastering the forces of dark, mechanical necessity that were engulfing society.

The conflict between the two conceptions, to which I have referred, came to a head at the first national conference, which was held in Leamington at Eastertide, 1934. There J. T. Murphy made his first appearance on a New Britain platform, being introduced with the specific object of injecting an upsetting element into the proceedings and bringing the conference to nought. For the movement was becoming too vigorous for Mitrinović and his inner circle to control. I blame the inner circle rather than Mitrinović himself for this, for they were always desperately anxious not to allow anything to get out of their hands. By a brilliant stroke, Mitrinović (behind the scenes, of course) imposed on the Conference with its overwhelming consent, a leadership of seven people, Col. J. V. Delahaye, J. T. Murphy, Professor Soddy, the Rev. A. D. Belden, H. T. F. Rhodes, Miss Gordon Fraser and myself. The voting in favour was about 120 to 17. Purdom said plainly that the new leadership was nonsense; and so it proved, for the leaders never once met or functioned in any way whatever. He made an eloquent protest against the proceedings, but he was publicly ignored, though privately Mitrinović made much of him. However, he was highly displeased by the whole affair, because, he said, it robbed the paper of serious purpose, and he resigned its editorship. This was virtually the end of the growth of the movement on a national basis. The shock was too great. Then for six months, until the end of August, I sat in the editorial chair. To sit was all I did. I was editor only in name. The real editor was Mitrinović. But it was a valuable experience. I learnt how to run a weekly journal.

I had a free hand in my own contributions, but that was all. For the rest, I was given all the copy that had to go in. I wrote something or other every week, mostly articles dealing with industrial, economic and financial questions. I also wrote many reviews. Beside all this, I continued to fulfil speaking engagements all over the country, so that I was kept busy.

But what a nightmare! The paper had exhausted its initial funds, so that it experienced increasingly enormous difficulty in keeping alive, and its circulation went catastrophically down. We literally did not know from week to week whether the next number would appear or not. I was not initiated into the mystery of the paper's finance; but on occasions I was asked to accompany a few people to interview some wealthy or influential person. Among many others I went to see the late Lord Allen of Hurtwood. He was very charming, but I came away empty-handed. There would be weeks when salaries were delayed. Towards the end, the money for printing had to be found for each issue before the printer would put it on the machine. Many a time I was informed at luncheon hour on the Monday (when we went to press) that there was no money to print. Miraculously it turned up. The financial uncertainty, my growing sense of the futility of the whole thing, my increasing friction with Mitrinović himself—all these combined to incur my desire to get free.

Gradually, relentlessly, my hopes and ambitions were turning into dust and ashes. All the day-dreams of being a figure of national importance were vanishing into miserable, frigid reality. I began to feel that I was being condemned to eddy around in the dizzy circumlocutions of this strange man, Mitrinović. I suddenly felt a loathing for the whole situation. I was becoming obsessed with the feeling that I was a failure. Earlier in the year, my wife had died, and her death had left me remorseful. After we settled in London we drifted apart. We ceased to be the companions and comrades we had been in Southport. But a few months before she died, I was suddenly made to realize that she was lonely and suffering and I spent every moment I could with her. During her last months, I nursed her night by night. I had a day nurse to look after her, and at night, when I returned from my meetings, I looked after her. We had come together again, but only to be parted by death. We learn too late. My grief served to aggravate my sense of failure and futility.

Although at first, and before the paper was issued, my contact with C. B. Purdom was hostile, for we had entirely different outlooks, we were destined to become firm friends. At first, he refused point blank to let me appear in the paper. Mitrinović brought us together and made us firm friends, more firmly indeed than perhaps he realized. I say that with some hesitation, for I doubt if there was anything that happened among those around him of which Mitrinović was not aware. He had the most uncanny insight. Later on C.B. spent a lot of time and trouble helping me in my writing. Of the hundreds of letters of congratulations I received on the success of my first book, *On To Orthodoxy*, none gave me greater pleasure than his.

There was one other significant memory of C.B. His secretary, Miss Ruth McCormick, became my second wife. When I succeeded him as editor of *New Britain* she became my secretary. Her father was Dr. G. S. McCormick, who had a medical practice in London, but had been dead for some years; her mother was both intellectual and an artist. The day after we got engaged I went at once to tell him that Ruth and I were going to be married: this was even before I told Mitrinović. He thought I was joking Then he laughed. I do not know to this day what passed through his mind at that moment. Whatever it was, to-day my wife and I have no better or more affectionate friends than he and his wife, Antonia.

My editorship of the paper ended at the second conference of what remained of the movement held in Glastonbury. For all practical purposes, that conference degenerated into a domestic conclave, and my connection with the movement became fitful and irregular. What was once New Britain dwindled into a personal, semi-spiritual fraternity, which toyed with the idea of political activity, which sought to effect political action by personal influence and contacts, and by trying to rope prominent individuals into the Mitrinović circle. In this way, contacts were made with trade union leaders, with members of parliament, with leading figures in business, journalism and culture. As I have stated, my connection with this was fractional. I was in-and-out or half-and-half, but sufficiently close to meet most of these prominent figures, both in England and France. We had a sort of working relation with the *Ordre Nouveau* in Paris, which meant that sometimes Mitrinović sent me to that city.

I shared with the average man the illusion that leaders in politics and other spheres were individuals of great knowledge, vision, wisdom and character. Constant contact with them throughout many years effectively cured me of that illusion, and for that among many other things besides, I am grateful to Mitrinović. With few exceptions I found them to be an inflation of the average, with very little qualitative difference. Egotism and vanity are what especially seem to mark them.

In September, 1938, I ended my association with the Mitrinović circle. I was voyaging on different waters.

CHAPTER IX

JUSTIFICATION BY PSYCHO-ANALYSIS

BEFORE I LEAVE the Mitrinović episode in my life and my painful search for myself, I must deal at some length with my specific psychological experiences of that time, for they have bearing upon it. One of the most striking features of modern thought, certainly since the opening of this century, has been the growth of psychology. Not one of the sciences has been so much the subject of both large and technical and small and popular manuals as psychology and its therapeutic development. In psychology, more especially in psycho-analysis, humanism reached the apex of arrogance and its deepest self-delusion, for men came to believe that in psychology they had, at last, reduced the redemption of mankind to a science. Psycho-analysis, it seemed, had achieved a comprehensive formula, according to which men could be made automatically good. At least, when perfected, the success of that formula could be guaranteed. Science had for all practical purposes abolished physical plague; psychology would abolish moral plagues no less surely. The great thing was to make men rationally aware of the sources of their fears and inhibitions, and lo! their anti-social will, their pride and egotism would vanish. That man is governed by an ultimate irrational will to self-assertion, which no human science can cure, is inconceivable by the modern mind, especially under the influence of psycho-analysis.

Being a true child of my time, I caught this infection. It was impossible to be in the Mitrinović ménage without getting the germ in its most virulent form. We all psychologized. There is no doubt that Mitrinović was deeply read in Freud and Jung and all the schools. His particular attachment was to Adler. How often did I hear him tell people their exact psychological status, as he had described mine. I remember him announcing to Delahaye what his trouble was. Delahaye turned to me and said: "David, do you understand that?" I did not, but I was not ready to admit it. What it meant in Delahaye was "father-complex". The women mostly suffered from "masculine protest". J. B. Boothroyd said to me once that Mitrinović's neurosis was the size of Nelson's column, and its name "synthesis".

I

Mitrinović, of course, was attempting the impossible. I do not think the worse of him for that. He was aiming at a new type of community, which should itself be a family. As part of his comprehensive political vision, it was magnificent in its sweep and daring. He desired to create an indissoluble community of people who should be, at one and the same time, nonentities, yet independent persons, each a "senator" as he called them. There was to be a socialized consciousness, each member to merge his self-consciousness with that of every other, yet retaining his own individuality, ". . . dividing the substance" though "not confounding the persons". He made all his intimates study the Athanasian Creed. He aimed at the socialized family of self-conscious individuals; one stream of consciousness, individually, uniquely realized. In short, he was trying to create the Kingdom of Heaven. That is, he was attempting the utterly impossible.

Since it was to be a community of real persons, it was necessary to get at the basic ego, which was very different from what we thought it was in ourselves. Our vision of ourselves was false and distorted. We were a mass of self-deceptions. These self-deceptions, like masks covering the ultimate self, had to be torn away. Then we should know ourselves and one another as we truly were. "Now we see in a glass darkly, but then face to face." This was step number one.

Each person entering on this discipline had to promise two things: first, always to tell the truth; second, never to resent truth-speaking from others about himself. I undertook with the others that when we met together we should engage in "group work", i.e. practise this discipline of discovering our true selves—to answer truthfully *all* questions put to one and to say truthfully what one felt about oneself and others; also to forgive, "to swallow my reactions", not to feel resentment at the truth speaking of others. Blissful ignoramus that I was! First, I did not speak the truth. Second, I deeply resented the truth from others. Third, others did not speak the truth. Fourth, they, too, resented the truth.

The technique was simple. Six or seven of us would meet for a session of three or four hours, generally late at night, for one's unconscious was supposed to be less remote in the deep night. One of the group would start, perhaps, by criticizing something I had done—a speech I had made, or the way I had behaved on some particular occasion. Against that criticism I would defend myself. By this time we were fairly launched, and gradually were out in deep waters. A member of the group would then say, in language that lacked nothing of brutality and candour, exactly what he, more frequently she (which made it worse!), thought of me. I was an unprincipled liar; or a shallow, pretentious poseur; a hollow, insincere tub-thumper; an impossibly vain, egotistic trumpet; a rogue; a twister. And much else.

"What about yourself?" I generally answered. Adept at the art of stringing words together I did not ask myself, what I really thought. I merely replied out of the anger and resentment aroused in me by the "truth-speaking". Many of the things said to me were true, and I knew they were true. But the spirit in which they were said was rarely truthful. Frequently those group-meetings ended in electric storms. After they closed, we all made our way to a café, generally Lyons' Corner House, because it was open all night, for a meal, and the atmosphere cooled down. We were good friends once more.

Let the reader bear in mind that these group-meetings took place at the end of a long day of varied activities. They continued from midnight to early morning. They soon acquired for me a compulsory element. I came to the point of utterly loathing them, and stayed away as often as I could. But Mitrinović attached the very greatest importance to them, and found ways and means of causing me to feel that I had to attend them. The consequence was that I developed a guilt feeling whenever I absented myself, except when I deliberately had an "outing", which happened with increasing frequency. Sometimes I cleared away from London, where no member of the circle could get at me. We never got anywhere with these meetings, with one important exception of which I shall tell presently. They were devoid of anything like method. We started anywhere and arrived nowhere. And always the same thing—accusations and recriminations. There were times when I hated the group-members—and Mitrinović most of all.

Generally these group-meetings were held without him, but occasionally he would attend and do the "grouping". It was a hateful business. These special group-meetings were much larger than the ordinary ones, as many as twenty or thirty being present. One person would usually be singled out for grouping. I was that hapless victim on numerous occasions. Mitrinović, of course, dictated the line of procedure, which the rest followed like tigerish sheep. He had a way of penetrating one's last defences, of peeling off, not only one's clothes, but one's skin, and flaying one alive.

Just as his masterly flattery made for ecstasy, so his equally masterly criticism made for torment. On these occasions, I cannot recall any one ever disagreeing with him or protesting. What Mitrinović said was the infrangible truth. The whole twenty or thirty (whatever their number) would take up the theme of Mitrinović's attack, and play variations upon it. The victim was helpless. He was battered (psychically) into stupidity. But—amazing man!—he had a marvellous way of dissipating the hatred. At the end of the session (four, five, six hours), he would whisk me off in a taxi to a restaurant, and then explain that he was subjecting me to all this process, because I was important, because I was strong. He left the weaklings alone, he said; but I was destined to play a great part, therefore I must be disciplined, purified, hardened. Whom the Master loveth "He also chasteneth". He rubbed salve into my wounds and soothed my vanity. For a time I responded to this treatment, and at the next performance gritted my teeth.

Let me make it clear that Mitrinović was sincerely convinced of the necessity of his methods. I am also convinced, however, that the whole affair gave him a certain amount of pleasure. Like all human beings, he was a mixture. But a mixture on the gigantic scale. He was wholly devoted to his task of creating his community, from which he rested neither day nor night. I cannot believe that he deluded himself to the extent of thinking that he was successful. I am certain, in any case, that he was no nearer creating a community of independent persons after thirty-six years in England, when he died, than he was when he started in 1914. The best people in his circle—and they are remarkably fine people—became, with hardly an exception, his echoes, subservient to him. He always declared that he wanted equals around him, and disclaimed the desire for yes-men. In fact his followers are yessers. I was never one of the inner circle, though Mitrinović sometimes made me think so. Neither was Purdom, because he was too critical and independent minded: but he always knew he was not, I believe. Of course there was never any possibility of Murphy being in it.

The atmosphere created by those around Mitrinović made independent co-operation impossible. They took it for granted that every suggestion and proposal made by him was agreed to by everybody; there was never any discussion of the proposal itself, only of how it was to be carried out. In September, 1938, for instance, he sent for me to say that he was sending telegrams to Mussolini and Hitler and others urging the peaceful cession of Sudetenland. That was his method.

I persevered more or less regularly under this discipline for something like five out of the seven years I spent with Mitrinović, so that it could not be justly denied that I gave it an extended trial, and the conclusion is that we most emphatically failed to create a community of united truth-telling, forgiving people. I never communicated to the group my deepest thoughts, if they differed from Mitrinović's. There was always an atmosphere of passionate attachment to a certain set of ideas and emotions, which we were supposed to think and feel. The expression of doubts was never shared. I tried it a few times, but it never worked.

I must admit, however, that Mitrinović himself would take infinite pains with individuals and allowed nothing to put him off. On one occasion, Watson Thompson had to go home to Edinburgh with malaria. Mitrinović travelled all the way North to see him. No trouble was too great for the cultivation of the person. But, in the last analysis, each person was an instrument. In saying this I may be doing him an injustice, but that was the feeling I had after my association with him. He took infinite pains with me and put up with endless disappointments, in the hope, I believe, that I would reach 100 per cent. agreement with him. The one thing he would not do was to allow one to remain as one was. He was always wanting to remake one in his own image. After seven years of persistent ceaseless effort with me, he gave it up as a bad job. At least, that is what I say, though in fact I gave it up myself; but I knew long before I left him that we should part company. During the last two years, I was in constant revolt. He knew I did not agree. On a point like that, you could not deceive him. Yet there was not a trace of malice in him or any bitterness. Never have I met anybody more free of either. I had two dreadful scenes with him when I accused him of all sorts of things and in great anger told him to go to hell. But it made no difference to Mitrinović, except that he afterwards made a greater fuss of me than ever. It was on the few occasions when I stood up to him that he held most tightly to me.

The attempt at general truth-speaking and forgiveness in the group was an utter failure. It bred a dangerous self-deception and a peculiar kind of hypocrisy. But it did one thing for me, for which I shall not cease to be grateful. It enabled me to listen to unpleasant truth about myself, and to realize that I was never so good as I thought I was; that there is always some element of egotism and unworthiness in my behaviour to which I am blind. I learnt to suffer acid criticism in the knowledge that I should discover the hitherto unsuspected element. Five years of that discipline convinced me that I can never be completely objective either about myself or about other people. It is a great thing to learn that in the very rancour and bitterness of people towards one there is an element of truth, to which one is wise to pay heed. I should never have learnt that without Mitrinović's group-work, and his searing castigations. A cruel and often unendurable process, it was a healing surgery. To feel the razor-edge of Mitrinović's insight into my soul was, I am sure, worth the pain. I believe I am a better man for it. Each time I ran away I said I would never go back. But I did go back and I am glad that I did, until the day came when I knew that I had exhausted the process, and passed on to new disciplines.

2

During this period I was psycho-analysed by four different practitioners—one a professional, the other three amateurs, more or less capable. None of this solved a single one of my problems, and my fundamental problem was not touched at all. No explanation of the sources of my restlessness, my instability, my temperamental fluctuations, gave me security of mind, steadiness of purpose or equilibrium. If anything, I was worse after each analysis. It was rather like the rheumatism from which I had suffered earlier when I began my hydropathic treatment, for before it I was able to walk: when it finished I was crippled. I had been assured that a course of analysis would solve many of my problems. It did not solve one. I was the same unregenerate old Adam after the exhaustive poking about in the bottom layers of my unconscious, as before. The uncovering of a man's complexes is not redemption.

In the course of these years with Mitrinović, I came into intimate contact with scores of people who were considered to be neurotic by themselves and others. Each had raked up a malodorous mess, only to remain the same frustrated, defeated being. I do not recall one person who emerged from analysis with the victor's crown. What I do remember is a ludicrous continuation of the process of disintegration and futile living. It imprisoned people in self-obsession.

I am not such a fool as to dismiss psycho-analysis. It has its place which seems to me to be much less therapeutic than diagnostic. The malaise of the soul does not lend itself to *scientific* treatment. Theology is more relevant than science. I learnt a great deal both from the practice and the theory of psychology in those hectic, absorbing years. If I were to put in summary form what I learnt, I should say that abnormal psychology, from which we all suffer more or less, is a demonstration of the mechanism of a deep-seated will to self-destruction.

Calvin knew this long before Freud; he called it by a different name. He knew it as Original Sin. And long before Calvin, about 620 years before Christ, Jeremiah knew the same thing. "For the heart of man is desperately sick." (xvii v.5). Or, as Dr. Skinner translates it, "The heart of man is beyond cure." The psychology of the later schools is an extraordinary confirmation of the Biblical view of man as a fallen creature.

This experience most effectively cured me of the illusion of psychology as a redemptive instrument, even if it cured me of nothing else. Consequently I reacted violently away from all this personal probing, from obsession with one's own neurosis and individual dissatisfactions. I began to long for Mitrinović to drop all this group-work; to abandon his Utopian quest of a new community, and get down to the brass-tacks of organizing a movement to win support for a political programme. At least let him release me to get on with the plain, practical work of converting opinion, without bothering about the discovery of the ultimate ego. If he wanted to persist in that, it was his own affair. But I was finally determined that I was not going to swim any more in the troubled waters of psychology.

But to give up his dream of the new family and community was the one thing Mitrinović would not do. I became more than ever conscious that my life was divided into two conflicting activities. During the day I followed my own inclination in the pursuit of politics. At night, much against my will, I was involved in the hunt for the ultimate ego. Pull devil pull baker. At all costs I would get clear of this; and I did.

3

The collapse of my hopes in this association with Mitrinović, which I have described at such length, meant the first descending steps into the deepest valley of the shadow. I had no star by which to steer. I no longer thought of social change in religious terms. I was purely secularist, "left alone with man". For all practical purposes, I had become atheist. I suppose if I had been asked point blank, "Do you believe in God?" I should have said, "Yes." But I never thought of God. God had ceased to mean anything to me. Even when my first wife died, I did not think of seeking consolation in religion, and my second marriage was at a registry office, a purely secular affair. As a practical present influence, even dimly, religion did not count with me. By this I mean that my consciousness had lost its sense of awareness of anything but humanity, this world, the concrete totality of things. To this typical modern mind, the God of the Bible has become utterly irrelevant. He is no part of "the universe of reference", any more than hobgoblins. Hobgoblins, fairies, demons—all such things to an average mind are part of a fantastic, non-existent world, never thought of as elements of reality. That was the mind which by this time I had become.

The idealist urge to build a new world had been swamped in my growing sense of the danger besetting our civilization. In this, too, I was typical of the modern secularist mind, especially the left-wing mind. The fine frenzy arising out of an exuberant, *positive* will to fashion a new order evaporated in the realization that the secure, established heritage of previous struggle was in danger of being lost. My concern now was not a new Socialist order, but the preservation of democracy; ordinary, bourgeois capitalist democracy. It is going to take us all our time, I thought, to keep what we've got. I was acutely alive to the menace of Fascism, still more to the menace of Hitlerism. The world is retreating, I felt. My whole being was pitched in a low key. Hitherto I had been crying for the moon. Now I began to cry for the street-lamp, which barbarian hands were seeking to destroy. I never had any illusions about the meaning of Hitler. I had read *Mein Kampf* long before the statesmen of the National Government had heard of the title. And I knew deep down inside myself, intuitively, that here was the destroying barbarian which Europe had bred within her bosom.

I was becoming sceptical about any new world. How can we get a new world, if we cannot summon the will and the energy to safeguard the few good things in the old world?

Significant living narrowed down to desperate defence of the *status quo*. I had no avenue of escape. Religion had ceased to count. And I could not live in the ivory tower of music and psychology.

From my first vision of the Kingdom of God as capable of earthly realization (with which I began my ministerial career), I had come to this obsession with the preservation of existing institutions! Bit by bit my idealism was withering away.

CHAPTER X

IN THE SCHOOL OF MARX

AMONG THE INFLUENCES that co-operated in driving me out of the orbit of Mitrinović was that of my wife. Ruth McCormick was a sensible, practically-minded, highly-efficient and generous girl, who saw what was happening to me and was anxious that I should sever my connection with Mitrinović altogether. Deeply religious herself, her desires intensified my own determination.

The second influence was my friendship with Col. J. A. Delahaye, and J. T. Murphy, the one-time communist, both seasoned politicians. Delahaye had preceded me in New Britain, Murphy followed me. Delahaye was a very untypical professional soldier, much too intelligent and catholic in his interests to gain favour with the authorities. Besides, he was a Socialist and had contested several constituencies. We became very close friends. He acted as best man at my wedding. J. T. Murphy was a professional agitator and revolutionary, a man of strong character and immovable convictions. He had had a stormy career. In the war of 1914–18, he was a pioneer leader of the Shop Stewards' Movement, which gave so much trouble to the Government. Later he became one of the leaders of the newly-founded Communist Party of Great Britain. In that capacity he went to Russia after the Bolshevik revolution and worked with Lenin in the Third International. On his return to England, he spent six months in prison on a charge of sedition. Later he broke with the Communist Party and became a free-lance socialist. I first met him as a contributor to the *Quarterly* I had "edited".

He was a convinced Marxist, but a Marxist of the better sort. He did his own thinking. He was sturdy, rugged, independent. Orage said of him that he wrote with his fist. He came to influence me very greatly, a fighter to his finger-tips, and of headstrong courage. Of all the men I have met, there is no one whom I would prefer to have with me in a battle. He would be the last to surrender. His loyalty to his convictions has cost him dear. He was a man of great ability, one of the ablest of British Marxists. He helped to convert me to Marxism. Strangely enough, it was he who gave me a book by Reinhold Niebuhr, *Reflections on the End of an Era*, which initiated the process that ultimately led me out of Marxism to orthodox Christianity.

In New Britain, into which he entered after the Leamington split, Murphy was always insisting on orthodox political action. He was the one man I ever knew in the Mitrinović circle on whom the latter never attempted any psychology. Murphy never hesitated to speak his Marxist mind. Mitrinović invariably agreed with him, but did not act on his suggestions. I found myself more and more acting with him and Delahaye.

One of the perennial themes of the pulpit is man's need of a faith by which to live. I had proved the truth of this in my experience. I was continually driven to seek something, not yet in being, with which I could identify myself. When my modernist gospel collapsed, I extracted its social essence, clothed it in Socialism and made that do as a faith. When Socialism as presented in the Labour Movement ceased to hold me, after the temporary diversion of music, I saw the vision of a New Europe and a New Britain through the powerful prism of the personality of Mitrinović. But by 1936 that ideal had ceased to be a faith and had become an irritant. This was my state of mind when J. T. Murphy's influence became decisive.

Murphy was at this time an active member of the Socialist League and shortly after I met him became its general secretary. Under his influence both Delahaye and I became very active members of this organization. The Socialist

League had been formed of a group of the I.L.P. who refused to follow the leadership of James Maxton outside the Labour Party, and was born of the revolt of socialist intellectuals to the course pursued by J. Ramsay MacDonald and the small group supporting the great betrayal of the Labour Movement in 1931, and MacDonald's desertion to become leader of the National Government.

Sir Stafford Cripps, K.C., who had not been long in the political arena as a member of Parliament, was chairman of the League. His interest in politics had been a churchman's interest in world peace, and for some years he had been a leading lay spokesman in the Church of England for the peace of the world to be secured through the League of Nations. Disillusioned by the response of the churches to successive campaigns he plunged into Labour politics, was quickly found a parliamentary constituency, elected to Parliament, and became Solicitor General of the second Labour Government. He had of course refused to follow MacDonald.

The prime mover in the founding of the Socialist League was Frank Wise, who died about a year after it was formed. He was a prominent member of the I.L.P. in the years when MacDonald was its leader. Cripps quickly established himself as the League's leading figure despite his immaturity as a political leader—primarily, perhaps, because he was its main financial supporter. Cripps was a great democrat when democracy agreed with Sir Stafford: when it did not, his support waned, or threatened to do so. He was, as all the world knows, a brilliant lawyer, a great churchman, very sincere, but very naïve in his evaluation of people and politics. He took his leadership for granted, and through all his charm shone a sort of patronage which sometimes annoyed me. He always spoke as to an intellectualized brief, rarely did he "let the heart speak" also. An excellent lucid, legalistic speaker, he was never warm, and therefore never an orator.

The executive committee contained a number of well-known socialists. At first, Clement Attlee, in pacifist mood, and deeply resenting the MacDonald split, Aneurin Bevan, G. S. Strauss, William Mellor, Frank Horrabin, H. N. Brailsford, and more of their calibre. J. T. Murphy as general secretary had no vote on the executive although participating in its discussions. His appointment strengthened the Marxist elements, but the Marxist who influenced Cripps most was William Mellor. He appeared to think himself free to function as a doctrinaire, and let himself go in the League, having no scope for doctrine in his job as editor of the *Daily Herald*. I hold him responsible for the Marxist indoctrination of Cripps during the period of its existence, not Murphy. Mellor was a powerful speaker, at his best a first-class orator, and a pungent writer as a journalist. He had once played an important role in the Guild Socialist Movement.

I got to know these men well and admired them, but it was Murphy who had inspired me to make myself thoroughly acquainted with Marxism, and it was in these days of my close association with him that I began to study Marx thoroughly.

Marxism is really a great world religion of the twentieth century. Its appeal has been extraordinary, and, in the early thirties, with Soviet Russia's achievements firing the idealism of the young people of Western Europe, its doctrines appealed also to many intellectuals in universities and political movements. In Russia, Marxism was making a new world: why not in Britain? Marxism appealed to a different part of society from that which worshipped at the altars of Freud and Jung. Marxism attracted the extrovert as distinct from the introvert. Perhaps I was exceptional in having felt the appeal of both.

Marxism came to assume for me the significance and proportions of a holy revelation. It became the "word" for the world, in which lay its salvation. So I settled down to a thorough study of Marx's *Capital*—the American edition (Charles Kerr) in three volumes. I am one of the by no means numerous band that has read the entire *three* volumes. I once asked T. A. Jackson, the author of *Dialectics* and one of the best-known British Marxists, how many people in Great Britain had read the three volumes. He doubted whether they numbered fifty! I don't know whether it is a matter for pride, but it is a fact that I have read many of those celebrated books of the world that are more talked about than read. For many years I made it a practice to read one world book every winter, and got through Plato's *Republic*, Dante's *Divine Comedy*, Milton's *Paradise Lost* and *Paradise Regained*, St. Augustine's *City of God*, Gibbon's *Decline and Fall of the Roman Empire* and many others. It took me nearly a year to read *Capital*, but I read it thoroughly, and summarized the whole of the first volume, which is the only one that Marx himself wrote in its entirety; the other two were largely written by Engels from Marx's material. I had the very great advantage of being able to discuss difficult points with Murphy, who knew his Marx thoroughly.

Capital has the reputation of being a difficult book to read. It is, certainly, not easy, but there are books I found much more difficult, even in economics—for example Keynes' two volumes on monetary theory, and Marshall's *Economics of Industry*. I found all the so-called Austrian school much harder going. Once I mastered what Marx meant by "community", "socially necessary labour-power", "surplus value", "variable and constant capital", I had little difficulty. I may even say that I enjoyed it. I do not agree that Marx's writing is heavy and laboured. There are passages of moving passion in *Capital*. There is, for instance, his description of the expropriation of the Scottish crofter. Even now, in spite of the much greater abominations that have been inflicted on the weak and defenceless, it has power to move me to indignation. Once I had got over the hurdle of the first few hundred pages, I found *Capital* comparatively smooth going.

I am of the opinion that Marx's basic economic concept, the labour theory of value, is essentially sound. That theory asserts that what constitutes the economic value of commodities is the amount of socially necessary labour power embodied in them. This is, I believe, truer to the facts even of contemporary capitalism than its Austrian competitor, that value is determined by the relation between supply and demand.

The outstanding things I learnt were, first, the exact mechanism of the exploitation of Labour; second, the nature of the contradiction inherent in Capitalism; third, the historic function of Capitalism and its exhaustion of that function; fourth, its consequent inevitable collapse.

Like nearly all non-Marxian Socialists, contemptuously referred to as "Utopian Socialists" by the Marxists, I had believed that capitalists sold goods for more than their worth. Marx showed me that goods were sold at cost. What really happened was that the capitalist paid to the worker less than the value of what he had produced. He appropriated to himself out of the price a portion of what was due to the worker. That was the surplus value, the excess over what the worker got, always less than the total value which the worker creates. So price equalled, not cost of production plus profit but cost of production minus a portion of the workers' value. This is the surplus value distributed in rent, interest and profit. Marx explained the mechanics of the process by which the workers are exploited. He also showed how they can never, under any system, be paid the full value of their labour. Part of it must always be retained for social services, renewal of plant, etc.; but the retention, he declared, must be controlled by society, not by a class of private owners.

The division of capital into variable and constant enabled me to see the contradiction inherent in capitalist production.

By "variable capital" Marx meant that portion of it which went to paying the human element in production, wages and salaries. This was variable, because its value increased. It is only the worker (i.e. the human factor) that creates new value. "Constant capital" was the raw material, machinery, etc., whose value never varied. This element in capital merely transfers its value unchanged into the commodities produced; it is, therefore, constant. Now, in the development of capitalism, the constant tends to gain at the expense of the variable, so the amount of surplus value tends to decrease since new value comes only from the variable capital. This is the contradiction in capitalism which in contemporary economics, has come to be known as "technological unemployment". The progressive displacement of labour by power machinery, which reduces purchasing power, is exactly what Marx described as the tendency of constant capital to increase at the expense of variable capital. It results in what Winston Churchill called "the curse of poverty in the midst of plenty", which Marx anticipated in what he described as "the increasing misery of the proletariat". This contradiction is of the essence of capitalism. There is no way of getting rid of it except by getting rid of capitalism.

Paradoxical as it may seem, Marx enabled me to see the virtue of capitalism. As an idealist, ethical socialist, I had seen no good at all in the system. It was completely evil. But I began to realize, as I read on, that capitalism had rendered great service to social progress by its immense increase of productive capacity. It had created the technical power to abolish poverty. But it had now exhausted its contribution to progress, for the simple reason that it was no longer developing productive power; on the contrary, it was beginning to hold it back. So I learnt that the test of the historic worth of a civilization was its ability to increase labour productivity. Involved in such increase also was the development of society and culture. A system that could no longer increase productive power was historically doomed. That, said Marx, was the certain fate of capitalism.

But *Capital* was only one of my studies at this time, though certainly the most important, for I plunged into the entire field of Marxism. I found it immensely stimulating and exciting, like entering a new world. I experienced a certain quality of ecstasy in my enthusiasm for Marxism, which I was to experience more strongly later in my re-discovery of the Bible. I can, without exaggeration, compare it to being in love. A grim mistress to be in love with, no doubt, but to the lover, the loved, however ugly and forbidding, is always beautiful. So was Marxism to me in my period of discovery. I can still re-live the impatience I felt, after meetings, to hasten back to the books. Literally for months, I read through the night hours until early dawn. It was a wonderful experience. London, with all its attractions, held no excitement comparable to it.

Engels I read with even greater enjoyment than Marx. By the time I came to him, I had a workmanlike grasp of Marxism in its threefold aspects—economic theory, meta-physics and philosophy of history, the last the supreme revelation. In *Anti-Dühring* and *Dialectical Materialism*, Engels made Historical Materialism crystal clear. I came to pity people who had not yet been illuminated by the holy revelation. I see its limitations and its defects to-day, but am strongly of the opinion that ignorance of the theory is a handicap to any student of the modern scene; ministers and clergy as a class are woefully ignorant of it. If I should ever have a say in the theological training of candidates for the ministry, I shall most assuredly make Historical Materialism a compulsory study for third-year theological students. They will be all the better-equipped preachers for it. It is interesting, to say the least, that some of the most creative Christian thinkers of today have been deeply influenced by Marxism: Niebuhr, Berdyaev, Barth, Brunner and Paul Tillich.

After Marx and Engels, I came to Plekhanov's *Fundamental*

Problems of Marxism. He was the first of the Russians. After him came Lenin, Trotsky, Bukharin and Stalin. In my most fanatical pro-Russian phase, however, I found Stalin dull and platitudinous. Lenin and Trotsky and, to a lesser extent, Bukharin, were of a different calibre.

For nearly two years I read practically nothing but Marxist books in both French and English. I also consumed vast quantities of periodicals. And what I received I was also giving out at meetings, classes, and in pamphlets and articles. I even wrote a book on *Capitalism and the Fate of the Churches.* Mercifully, it was refused.

I

During my first year with the Socialist League it functioned entirely as a socialist propaganda organization, until Italy's attack on Abyssinia raised the issue of the League's attitude to the League of Nations, to war in general and the Italian war in particular. The Labour Movement, as indeed the whole country, was in an anti-war mood, committed to the League of Nations and its Covenant. The Socialist League held the view that war was the product of capitalism, and that the League of Nations was a capitalist institution which could not be used as an instrument of peace. When the Labour Party declared itself in favour of the League of Nations using sanctions against Italy, the Socialist League was in a fix. Composed of pacifists, marxists and romantic socialists, such as Cripps himself, it had to make up its mind whether the Labour Party's policy was to be supported. Should it function as a party or propaganda body? This was, indeed, part of the crisis facing the whole Labour Movement. World war was on the horizon and the Fascist powers were bringing it ever nearer. This was the international significance of the Italian-Abyssinian war. The Labour Party had not made up its mind about re-armament.

In this situation Sir Stafford Cripps lost his head! Mellor, the ex-communist, still held the view that the League of Nations was a capitalist organ. His policy, and Cripps', was to have nothing to do with the League, to oppose re-armament, and to unite the working class against war. The pacifists of the Socialist League felt they could support this line, and that the capitalist powers would line up behind the anti-comintern pact for war on Socialist Russia.

Murphy, who as a first-class Marxist used Marxism to think with, differed profoundly from his fellow Marxists in the League, but was held in such high regard by the League executive that when their resolutions were prepared for the Bristol conference he opposed them on all counts, and was allowed to submit alternative resolutions. In support of his proposals he made a most powerful speech, which I wished with all my heart I could have supported. (I was not a dele-gate.) He foreshadowed the alliance which ultimately came into being of the Allied Powers including Russia against the Axis powers; he said that Japan would choose her time, pursue her own policy, and make her own war of conquest; he supported the Labour Party's demand for sanctions against Italy and was in favour of re-armament and an alliance of all anti-Nazi and anti-Fascist powers. The execu-tive mobilized all its oratorical resources against Murphy, who had no opportunity to do more than state his case. He got no support, not one vote.

It was, however, from that conference and Murphy's isolated stand for a new, more realistic, policy that he, Delahaye and I moved from the Socialist League to a fresh campaign for what we called "a People's Front against Fascism". Immediately there came the famous Brighton Conference of the Labour Party where Ernest Bevin swept George Lansbury from the leadership of the Party, and thrashed Cripps and his supporters. Later Cripps came round to the People's Front position, i.e., a union of work-ing-class parties, with the Liberals and Conservatives, on a programme of resisting Fascism.

By this time, the vision of a new social order had faded from my mind, for the brutal realities of a degenerating Europe sponged it away. I felt something had gone wrong. The idea of an accumulating working-class will to revolutionize society was not working out. My concern now was not to establish a socialist England, but to preserve trade-unionism and the democratic rights and privileges which we had all thought to be secured for ever. I became obsessed by the power of Fascism and Nazism. I felt there was a too-easy-going optimism that "it can't happen here". Orthodox Labour was for a while very complacent. Orthodox Toryism toyed with the idea that Fascism might be a good thing. Some Liberals, even, admired Hitler, and Lloyd George warned the House of Commons to be careful not to oppose him too much, since he was the last bulwark in Germany against Communism. As events turned out, I was much more right about Hitlerism than those who dubbed me a scaremonger. Murphy resigned from the Socialist League, and I started to advocate this policy within the League, and was excommunicated for my pains.

2

The idea of a "people's front" was derived from the formation of the "Popular Front" in France which gave rise to the People's Front Government of Léon Blum. At this time too, Allen Young (a Marxist) was editing a journal with the "middle way" ideas sponsored by Macmillan and Butler, then regarded as left conservatives. This journal supported us; quickly we got together a group, and with Geoffrey Sainsbury, Allen Young, Le Gros Clark, and a few others, launched a campaign. We raised enough money to rent offices, first in Bloomsbury Street, then in the Strand, for a year, to pay a full-time secretary and two typists, to print scores of thousands of leaflets and pamphlets, and to organize conferences and hundreds of public meetings. We started from nothing. In addition, we formed local committees throughout London. I spoke to numerous organizations and came to know all sorts of people. It was an experience I should never have had in any other way. At a crowded meeting at the Friends' Meeting House, the other speakers beside myself were G. D. H. Cole, John Strachey, Richard Acland, and Robert Boothby. Canon Guy Rogers was in the chair. Boothby was so upset by some of the things Cole said that he walked off the platform. But big public meetings, of which this was one of many, were utterly useless.

The Peace Ballot of 1935 had revealed how great was the desire for peace, so that Baldwin dared not put his re-armament programme before the electorate in the election at the end of that year, and the Labour Party was divided on the issue of supporting re-armament. The confusion about the role of the British Government in world affairs, and especially towards war and peace, was great. We had no doubts in our own minds that this country had to prepare for war or go down to defeat before the Nazi offensive. But the Labour Conference was divided against itself, and Dalton would not have won through but for the powerful support of Ernest Bevin from the Trades Unions. This confusion on all sides meant that we, who had come forward with the bold proposition for popular unity at home and abroad irrespective of party or class loyalty against the most reactionary and destructive force of Nazism and Fascism, had little chance of success. The Communists demanded that unity of the working class should precede any unity with any other section of society. The Socialist League demanded the same. For the Communists this meant that a prior condition for unity of any kind was their affiliation to the Labour Party, which the Labour Party would not accept at any price. For the Socialist League, it meant violating the constitution of the Labour Party, which if persisted in would result in the expulsion of the League. Yet Stafford Cripps persisted until the Socialist League had to close down, and, finally, conducting a personal campaign, he was expelled with his prominent supporters, and when the war came was a member of no party at all.

As a committee we had worked a good deal with the Left-Book Club, and when our committee finally ceased, I did a great deal with the Club. Its initial success had been staggering, and brought Victor Gollancz dreams and visions. Its national organizer was a close personal friend, Dr. John Lewis, Unitarian minister at Ipswich, and my work with him brought personal contacts with the Communist Party and its leaders. I spoke frequently on the Party platform with Strachey, Ted Bramley, Professor Haldane, Wal Hannington and many others.

The Communist Party inspired extraordinary zeal and devotion. I reflected that in spite of, or because of, its authoritarian character, it commanded endless sacrifice. In less disciplined movements, there was far less enthusiasm. Was there—is there—a connection between discipline and devotion? There is a rough parallel (or there was) between the Communist Party and the primitive Church. Both were apocalyptic; both were ostracized; both commanded intense loyalty.

John Strachey was the ablest of the Communists, as Harry Pollitt was the most popular. But for all his intellectual capacity, Strachey is a man of extraordinary limitations. He sees nothing in religion except a social product.

Of course, I am speaking of years ago. Events may have twisted his Marxism, for if Joad could have wondered whether Original Sin may be somewhere near the truth, Strachey, too, may change in his view of religion. Harry Pollitt will not change—not that that is impossible, for I used to think that if Stalin had proclaimed Christianity to be true, Pollitt would have become a Christian the following day.

I was present once at a meeting of Left-Wing Marxist

parsons, addressed by Harry Pollitt. One of the parsons asked how a particular point which Pollitt had just made could be squared with Christianity. "Does that matter?" he asked. He then said he had taken it for granted that they (the parsons) did not really believe in the religion they preached! Though Mr. Pollitt has a lot to learn, one thing nobody can teach him is the art of popular oratory. Nobody can hold a crowd better than he.

3

These People's Front activities brought me into contact with Jack White, son of the General White who defended Ladysmith in the Boer War. Brought up in an ultra-bourgeois home, Jack cut loose and refused to be respectable. He had taken an active part in the training of the Irish citizen army in 1913, but by accident missed the rebellion of 1916.

Here let me relate one of my experiences in Hampstead where I first met Jack. Among my many jobs in the People's Front was to get hold of clergy and ministers. We prepared a statement for circulation to churches and I had to get the signatures of prominent ministers. With that object, I called upon the Rev. John Short, at Lyndhurst Road, Hampstead, after a morning service. I explained the object of my visit and submitted the statement. As he read, I could see his face stiffening. He said he did not believe in political activities. "It is not a People's Front the nation needs," he said. I enquired what then did people need. "To get down upon their knees," he answered. "But what do you suggest they should do when they get up from their knees?" Before I realized what was happening there was a fierce slanging match. Dr. Short could hand it out and did so with gusto. A few weeks later in the Tube at Belsize Park, I felt a hand on my shoulder. I turned round to hear a voice saying, "Excuse me, you are Mr. Davies?" It was Dr. Short. "We were rather childish the other Sunday, weren't we?" he remarked. He was charming and disarming, and invited me to call upon him, which I did. To cut a long story short, we became good friends and exchanged ideas. I talked to him about Marx, and he talked to me about Barth.

To return to Jack White. He told me about people he knew in London amongst whom was a packet of Marxist clergy in Islington. I was sufficiently intrigued to express the wish to meet them. Jack took me along, and I met Father (Bill) Iredell, vicar of St. Clement's, Barnsbury, and his curates, Stanley Evans and Leonard Schiff. I got them interested in the People's Front and they got me interested in St. Clement's. It was an extraordinary business. Bill used to close his services by raising his right fist, which was the People's Front sign, in front of the altar. He organized a series of special services after Evening Prayer at which addresses were given on Marxism and Christianity. He asked me to give one of them. On that occasion we sang either the Red Flag or the Internationale. Bill was passionately in earnest and acted according to his lights, which, I fear, were rather dim, both Christian and Marxist. Once again I marvelled at the elasticity of the Church of England. This was at the end of 1936 or the beginning of 1937. But in 1936 all our People's Front activities turned to the support of the Spanish Republic. Bill was profoundly moved over Spain, all honour to him. He preached on Spain, prayed for Spain, and organized collections at his church to help the People's Front Government—as he put it—to get machine guns. He asked me to draft a leaflet which he wanted to distribute to the bishops and clergy. Bit by bit I was drawn into his Spanish schemes.

Of course, I did not need any prodding on the great issue at stake in the Spanish Civil War. I grasped its significance with crystal clearness. Sir Samuel Hoare, with the lack of moral discernment which only a Cabinet Minister could display, had dismissed it as "a fight between two miserable factions", for in those fatal years, 1936-8, Britain was as blind as a bat. I grasped only too firmly that Spain was the second battlefield of the second World War. The first was Abyssinia.

Spain became the inspiring activity of People's Front propaganda, and, as our committee perished, the Spanish struggle absorbed my entire time and energy. The office of the Hampstead Spanish Aid Committee was housed in my flat in Hampstead, where my daughter Diana was born, and where, instead of a Christening service, I arranged a gathering to receive the babe into the human family, with Jack Murphy as representative of the People. So far had I gone from the Church. What Ruth thought of this, she did not say, and, though I was well aware that her religious faith had not dimmed, I ignored the fact.

Every night, somewhere or other, I was addressing meetings on Spain either for the Communist Party with which on this issue I co-operated closely, or the National Spanish Aid Committee. One morning, I got a telephone call from Bill Iredell. Was I prepared to go to Spain as a member of a delegation to investigate the relation of the People's Front Government to the Church? And whom could I suggest as members of such a delegation?

The Catholic papers, *The Universe* and *The Tablet*, were presenting the Civil War as a struggle in defence of Christianity. As the Archbishop of York said, in refreshingly unepiscopal language, "This is rubbish." But all is grist that comes to the Roman mill. Atrocity stories were retailed about the murder of priests, the raping of nuns, the desecration of churches, and the suppression of religion, a propaganda which undoubtedly gained much undeserved sympathy for Franco. The Republican Government felt that this propaganda should be counteracted. So they invited a competent delegation to come to Spain to investigate, with absolute freedom, the whole matter. Father Iredell was asked to organize the delegation, in which task he had the assistance of Mrs. Hannah Laurie.

A delegation was got together, which, owing to the presence on it of the Dean of Canterbury, came to be known as the Dean of Canterbury's Delegation. That was all to the good, though not exactly true, for at that time the Dean had not become known as the "Red Dean", but he threw over the delegation the mantle of considerability. His championing of Douglas Social Credit had gained him a certain notoriety, but not of such a character as to inspire horror in the breasts of the respectable. A puzzling clergyman perhaps, but not blasphemous—not yet. Other members were Professor Macmurray, Kenneth Ingram, a prominent Left Christian, two Catholic women, besides Bill Iredell, Mrs. Laurie and myself, also Miss Levertoff.

We were ready to go, when at the last moment the Foreign Office dropped a bombshell by announcing that it would not grant us passports. The Dean tried to get an interview with the Foreign Secretary, but he was out of town. On the Saturday we were informed that Sir George Mountsey, one of the permanent secretaries, would meet representatives of the delegation the following morning. So Mrs. Laurie and myself were deputed to meet him. This was my first meeting with any of the heads of the Foreign Office. It was most instructive. His manners were perfect. He was most courteous, especially when Mrs. Laurie was rude to him, as she was on several occasions, for she was adept at the curt word. Sir George remained most charming. He was prepared to do anything to help us, except let us go to Spain. He didn't put it like that: he was immensely concerned with our safety. After all there was a war on, and we might be hurt. His Majesty's Government were determined to see that *that* should not happen. He faintly hinted that the Civil War was a purely Spanish affair. He conveyed a distant echo of disapproval, all very beautifully done. One couldn't feel angry. He would consult His Majesty's Secretary of State for Foreign Affairs, but held out no hope.

Then, quite unaccountably, news came late on Monday

afternoon that permission had been granted; so I had my passport stamped: "Valid for Spain for one journey only." We were informed that we should also require French permission to travel to Spain. We decided to obtain that in Paris.

Little did I realize that my experiences in Spain would be the end of the faith by which, in different forms, I had lived since I had left the ministry in 1928. The humanist, self-sufficient hope of inevitable progress was rapidly disintegrating. My Marxism, too, was shaken. I had been reading Reinhold Niebuhr's *Reflections on the End of an Era*, one of those books whose effect is not realized till long after, like a wound in battle the hurt of which, hardly felt at the moment of its happening, becomes very painful later on. The book jolted me at several points, especially its criticism of Marxism, which underestimated, said Niebuhr, the *original sin* in man. That struck me hard at the moment, but its full meaning was not to dawn upon me till later. What impressed me was that here was a man of divinity who obviously knew Marx thoroughly. It was very unusual.

There was another factor—the Russian Trials, which first puzzled, then angered, and finally revolted me, for Russia was the home of my humanist faith and idealism; hence my reluctance, indeed my inability, to grasp the enormity of these trials. Gradually I was forced to face the dreadful truth. But not until I came back from Spain did the full realization of their dark iniquity come to me. Whether the wretched prisoners were guilty or not, one thing seemed to me to be certain, the satanic guilt of Stalin. In due course, I read the verbatim reports; I also read and re-read the report of the American Commission, under the chairmanship of John Dewey, which investigated the charges against Trotsky. In the light of the trials, Russia, this new world of my faith, was revealed as a naked horror and monstrosity. When I set out for Spain, I was more than half-way to the conclusion that man was incurably corrupt, that Utopia was beyond his power, and when in Spain I saw the horror and tragedy and bestiality of man, I was rapidly driven the rest of the way. On my journey to Spain I possessed a dying faith. On my return I brought back a corpse. Within a few months, despair had made my life an insupportable burden.

CHAPTER XI

SPANISH INTERLUDE

THE PARTY SET off that Monday evening in 1937 and we arrived without incident in Paris at 9 a.m. the following morning. The Foreign Office episode had given us a little notoriety, so at the Gare du Nord we were besieged by French pressmen. During our three-day wait in Paris we had plenty of publicity. After some formalities at the British Consulate, we were driven to the Spanish Embassy off the Champs-Elysées and met the Ambassador and his very charming wife. Luis Araquistain was the complete opposite of the British diplomat. A journalist by profession, a man of broad, deep culture, a Liberal in the best sense of the word, and a man of the people. There were no barriers to be thrown down, and he made contact and conversation easy. He was very ably seconded by Madame Araquistain. One of the things that impressed me at the Embassy was the friendly, easy relations with the domestic staff, who were treated as friends. And they treated us also as friends: it was a People's Embassy.

As the French authorities seemed reluctant to give us the necessary visas, we had to kick our heels in Paris for a few days. It was all of a piece. The People's Front Government in France, under a Socialist Premier, looked on at the life and death struggle of a sister democracy with folded arms. It frowned on any attempt to help. But at last we got what we had come for.

I

We decided to divide the delegation into two parts—one to go to Bilbao and the other to Madrid. I went to Bilbao,

169

together with the Dean, Macmurray and the two ladies. We were to join forces later at Valencia. So on Thursday night we left Paris at 8.0 p.m. for Toulouse. On the train was Claude Cockburn, editor of *The Week*, also Frank Pitcairn of *The Daily Worker*. The British Government had forbidden him to leave the country, but none the less he managed to get into Spain. There are always ways and means. We arrived in Toulouse at 6 a.m., where the Bilbao section had to change. From there we were to go by air.

At Toulouse there was another long wait. As we were supposed to depart at 10 a.m. we trooped off to the Cathedral, where (at 6.30 a.m.) Mass was in progress. Macmurray and I soon came away. "I can't associate all that muttering and genuflecting and bead-counting with religion," I remarked to Macmurray. "Neither can I," he replied. "A lot of mumbo-jumbo." Which considerably encouraged me. And while I feel very different about worship now from what I felt then, Roman worship, I confess, still leaves me cold. Strange to say, I have no such feeling at Greek Orthodox services, which are even more ornate and ceremonious. How glad I was to get out into the Toulouse fresh air! I have not seen all the French cathedrals, but of the many I have seen, Toulouse is the worst. Its interior is dingy, its statuary and furnishings cheaper than usual.

After breakfast at the station hotel, Macmurray nearly cleared the kiosk of matches. He did not intend to go short of them in Spain. I got a copy of the *Dépêche de Toulouse*, and read that newspaper all the morning, for we did not get away until 1.30 p.m. There was bad weather about, and we arrived at Santander at exactly 3.15, where we were motored to the Town Hall to meet the governing authorities of the town. I was struck at once with what impressed me wherever I went in Spain—the youth of the people in control. It was very rare indeed to see an old man among them. The President of the Basque Republic was about 34; the Foreign Secretary a young engineer in his twenties. The average age of the Basque Government was not much more than 30. It was, however, not the same in Madrid. There age was at the helm.

In the Santander (St. Andrew) province, which is not part of the Basque Republic, we noticed a few burnt churches. The Santander people frankly admitted that they had closed them for the safety of the realm and for that of the priests themselves. The burning was a spontaneous popular act, for the Church was hostile to the Republic. The Santander people found a priest for us to interview. He was in mufti. Priests, he said, dare not wear clerical garb, lest people in the street molest them, which seemed to suggest popular hostility. He admitted to the Dean that the Government left him alone, and said it was better that the church should be closed in the circumstances. In answer to a question he did not hesitate to say that he hoped Franco would win—in the presence of our Government interpreter. I could not imagine a priest in Russia saying in the hearing of a commissar that he hoped Stalin would be overthrown; or in Germany, Hitler. But this good man did not hesitate. My impression was that there was certainly no Government persecution.

Why is it, I asked myself, that when people revolt in Spain, outside the Basque country, it is the churches they first destroy? I can't imagine that happening in England, certainly not in Wales, where they would probably go first for banks and government buildings. A study of the history of the Catholic Church in Spain supplies the answer: it has always been against the people. Were I a Spaniard living under the harrow of an exploiting Church, I should hurl the faggots with the best of them.

The same evening we were taken by a young soldier to Bilbao, a distance of about 80 miles. I shall never forget that ride, for it was a nightmare: I thought every moment was my last. For the first time (and, I earnestly pray, the last) the sweat came out from beneath my finger-nails—a ghastly experience. The driver took the sharp turns in the road at a frenzied helter-skelter, rushed the descents and swooped the ascents. He raced the car as though he were pursued by all the demons from hell. In answer to my protests, the young madman laughed with a gay insouciance. He hadn't been driving *really* fast! How can one account for the addiction of continental motorists to reckless driving?

I summarize my experience in Bilbao in four points.

First, there was complete accord between the Government and the clergy, a condition that obtained nowhere else in Spain. The Church seemed to be one with the people in their struggle. One proof of this was the savage vengeance Franco afterwards took upon the Basque priesthood, many of them were butchered out of hand. That members of the Government were practising Catholics, we had many evidences. The President attended Mass every day. Another member who accompanied the Dean and myself to the front line one Saturday night, and did not return to Bilbao until 4 a.m., was at the 6 a.m. Mass. All the churches were open and conducting full ministrations. There were people present at all hours of the day and evening, sometimes in great numbers. I did not hear a single priest complain either of Government persecution or popular hostility. On the contrary, Church, people and Government were united. The explanation was that the Church among the Basques had a different history and attitude from that of the Church in the rest of Spain. It was forward in social activities among the people, and conducting some valuable social experiments in which the Government greatly interested itself. Even in the midst of the grievous torment of civil war, these experiments (in education, in the use of leisure, and so on) were not allowed to stop. Here the Church was not faced with the problem of how to get the people to church. The people were united with it. The description of the Roman Church was no exaggeration in Bilbao—"Our

Holy Mother Church". One could not fail to see it. And moreover, the Church was supporting the Government in its resistance to Franco.

Second, I observed that the Government was desperately trying to preserve in its daily practice the values which it went to war to defend. This was such a contrast to the practice of Russia, for example, that it intensified my already active doubts of the order upon which I had pinned my hopes. The Basques were humane in their treatment of opponents. For instance, we expressed a wish to visit the prison in which Fifth Columnists were imprisoned. We went, accompanied by the Minister of Justice. I was surprised at what I saw. We found men associated together in big rooms, conversing, reading, playing games, smoking. There was no solitary confinement. They occupied single cells only to sleep. There was no physical punishment. Within the prison there was freedom of movement. Men did not look cowed or beaten. They buttonholed the Minister and made their complaints to him personally, which I thought extraordinary. In the women's prison, we found women sewing and laughing together. The treatment meted out to prisoners contrasted greatly with the horrors that obtained in Fascist lands and, alas, in the one Socialist country. This behaviour was characteristic of the Basque Government in all its activities. Even in the midst of civil war, it pushed ahead with its new hospitals, its children's clinics, its new schools, its hopeful social experiments. We visited many of these and were greatly impressed. History will never know what the world missed by the defeat of these good people; for here was a Government that thought of greatness in terms of humanity and social welfare.

The third thing that came painfully home to my mind was the vast misery and suffering. Of course, one always knows of the existence of this in a remote way, but here the remote idea became flesh. It assumed the visible form of human beings. I passed through an experience in which I felt the magnitude of human frustration, pain and defeat. For a moment, I gathered up in myself the suffering of hungry, baffled men and women. It went a long way to push me to my final despair. One night, I walked alone through some of the back streets of Bilbao. In the deepening dusk, I saw men and women poking into rubbish cans, carefully picking out bits of refuse, in the hope that they could be made edible. People were perpetually hungry. Ourselves, we ate only fish and oranges, no meat, or bread or fats. Bilbao went through months of misery, lacking bread.

After a few days I was struck by the almost complete absence of dogs. It was very unusual. Every civilized community has a dog population. I remarked on it to our interpreter. "They've all been eaten," he replied. What vast misery and suffering the remark implied. Everything in the life of the city bore it out—empty shops, empty cafés. Only tobacco could be bought, but matches were unobtainable. Macmurray had been wise. It was an illuminating experience to live for a month in a community in which the most ordinary things were unobtainable—bread, matches, tea, coffee, chocolate.

Every night and all night, heavy lorries loaded with soldiers rumbled past my hotel on their way to the front. The thoughts created by the sound kept me awake through most of the night. Earlier in the day I had seen young men assembled in the barracks, preparatory to battle. The delegation had been taken on a visit to one of the training centres. There were thousands of youths, little more than boys, getting ready to fight against impossible odds. It was like speaking to condemned men, heavy with foreboding. Those days and nights in Bilbao were a Golgotha. But the deep night reverberations of the loaded lorries were even more eloquent to me in my troubled unrest. On that long and beautiful road to Durango and Eibar, under the looming shapes of the mountains, those fresh youths were driven in the lonely dark nearer and nearer their doom.

Something profound happened to me in those sleepless hours, something unrealized at the time. Those heavy sounds robbed me, not only of my sleep, but of my last remaining defences against the ultimate despair of the human soul. Those lorries pounded into dust some of my last pretences that all was well. Beyond my conscious cerebral processes, there was taking place a dying of spirit which was answering to the physical dying of men only twenty or thirty miles away. My hopes were flickering out in the darkness. A whole lifetime's optimism was disintegrating. Ere long, what happened in those endless nights emerged into consciousness, bringing the last despair that man can feel.

Fourth, these dim and inaccessible happenings in the depths of my being were greatly accentuated, I believe, by first-hand contacts with war. War is the greatest symbol of the inescapable impotence and contradiction of humanity. My direct contact with war in Spain was like shaking hands with Death. The feel of its clamminess dissolves any possible denial of death. That is what Spain did for me.

One Saturday night the delegation was entertained by the President of the Government. It was a good dinner, much too good to be served in a city of hungry multitudes. If delegations must visit stricken areas, let them at least fare no better than their hosts. A few days earlier, I had expressed the wish to visit the front line if that were possible. At the dinner, the President informed me that he was putting his own car and chauffeur at my disposal to take me to the front after the dinner was over. Spaniards dine very late. It was 1 a.m. when the last mouthful had been consumed. The Dean of Canterbury announced that he could not dream of letting me go to the front alone. I needed looking after!

Soon after one o'clock, we set off. Leaving Bilbao at a good pace, we soon had to slow down as we hit the Durango road. At intervals of a mile or less, we were pulled up by sentries who demanded papers. Some of these were women. It was a clear star-lit night. There seems to be a kind of suppressed light in the darkest hour of a Spanish night. We could see sufficiently well to make out the countryside, the remote mountain skyline and the silent houses. I felt a deep and weary sadness. As I stole a glance at the Dean huddled in his corner, I wondered what was passing through his mind.

Suddenly the car pulled up close to the roadside, and I saw the vanguard of a long procession. It still remains the saddest sight I have ever seen. It was living evidence of the brutality of human nature. It was a procession of weary, homeless men, women, children and animals, fleeing from the horrors of devastated Durango to a place of safety. Old men and women trudged stolidly along. Donkeys were loaded with household belongings. Women carried babies in their arms, and their menfolk had young children on their shoulders. There were hundreds in that procession. My mind went back to the prophecies of Isaiah and I pictured the heart-breaking trek of the Jewish exiles to Babylon. Here it was re-enacted under my eyes. I was sitting in a luxurious motor-car, a product of the twentieth century, the century of man's greatest triumphs, and here was the resurrected seventh century B.C. Side by side were man's creative genius and his sinful will; the symbol of man's control of Nature and his lack of control of human nature. It was at that moment that my belief in progress collapsed.

Before the melancholy column had passed our car, my vision had been blurred by tears streaming from my eyes. Neither the Dean nor I spoke. I could tell easily the pain and sorrow in his eyes, as he gazed on those stricken people. But nothing was said, and the car drove on into the night. Deep down, like a knife in the vitals, I knew that this scene was the prologue to the greater tragedy through which Europe was to pass. Poland, Belgium, France and Holland have since witnessed scenes that have eclipsed what I saw in satanic horror; scenes that tempt one to think that the ancients, compared with us moderns, were another and better humanity. It was on a Spanish roadside that the realization of man's incurable evil seized my heart.

We arrived at last at the forward posts. "I am now," I said to myself, "in the area of battle, where men are slaying one another." The thoughts made me tremble. A captain explained the situation to me. There—pointing on the map —are our front lines. Here are the enemy lines, only half a mile away. I heard firing, rifles were spitting venomous death. There were Moors in the line here. Was it possible to go into the trenches? The captain shrugged his shoulders, and it was explained that it was too risky. The Dean expostulated with me and urged that I should not press my desires on reluctant men. In the midst of the talk the telephone bell rang and there came the message that the attack had begun. At about 3 a.m. we were ushered away, for serious business was afoot. As we moved, we could hear the firing increasing in volume and flashes of flame licked the darkness. Then by a different route, we were taken through the little town of Eibar, famous for its manufacture of small firearms. It was a hopeless ruin, reduced to dust and rubble by heavy German and Italian artillery. Thence we returned to Bilbao. I felt numb, physically and morally exhausted. In my bedroom, before getting into bed, for the first time for years, I knelt down and cried: "Oh God!" That was all! But though I knew not God, that was, I believe, the deepest prayer I had ever uttered, the preliminary cry of utter despair. Into it was packed the failure of a lifetime.

This was the anti-climax of a long process. It penetrated into consciousness in my first air-raid. We were lunching at our Bilbao hotel when the siren went. I moved down to the shelter in the basement and confess that I was frightened. Too vividly I wondered whether this was to be the end. Later I grew rather blasé as so many of us did in those dreadful days and nights of German attack, but then I was as scared as a mouse. Strangely enough, after I had got safely to the shelter, I became absorbed in the sight of a young woman holding a baby, and for the moment forgot my own fear. My mind went instantly to the thought of my own little daughter, Diana, only 15 months old. And my heart ached with protective love. I thought, too, of my wife, and longed that I might love her. How easily, I thought, it might be that she too would be holding her baby in her arms in an air-raid: which actually happened later, scores of times. Often have I carried my little girl—a precious burden—down to the shelter, and comforted my wife, for whom love was to return. As I stood there in the basement of a Bilbao hotel, I saw in the eyes of that mother the vast, hungry, protective love of one human being for another. It was an ennobling, purifying spectacle.

My worse air-raid experience, however, was in Durango, when several churches were destroyed. It was Franco who burnt the churches in Northern Spain. Neither *The Universe* nor *The Tablet* made that the subject of leading articles. Franco announced after that raid that it was the Reds who fired the Durango churches, which was a dreadful lie. There were no Communists in Durango. As it happened, the delegation were eye-witnesses of that raid and saw the bombs drop. Within twenty minutes we reached the bombed area. We all signed a statement to that effect, and, that same evening, the Dean broadcast to the world an eye-witness account.

It was a lucky accident that prevented us from being in the actual target area. We were to have left Bilbao at 2.45 p.m. for Durango. But my desire to destroy Major Douglas' A + B Theorem, of the truth of which the Dean was mystically convinced, made us half an hour late. That probably saved our lives. Afterwards the Dean jocularly informed a Manchester audience in the Free Trade Hall that he owed his life to me. Had I been a Douglasite, I should not have entered into controversy with the Dean that afternoon, so we should have departed punctually and arrived in Durango in time to be bombed. However, we were on the outskirts of Durango when the raid started. But air bombardment has become so familiar a thing to English readers that a description is not necessary. Durango and its churches were destroyed by German and Italian 'planes whose presence in Spain was continually denied.

It was in Spain that I began to be aware of the ultimate implications of the loss of Christian faith. It had taken me over ten years. I was compressing into a decade the process and logic of the whole modern era, which began in the Renaissance with optimistic confidence in the omnipotence of collective man and was now entering on the paralysis of self-doubt and frustration. If I may symbolize this process in persons, I would say that the modern world had travelled from Pico della Mirandola to Martin Heidegger, from the dewy dawn of a naïve optimism to the gloom of a troubled pessimism. Like a seed growing unperceived and sprouting at last into the open, so the process of exhausting humanism had been going on in me for years unperceived. In Spain it stalked into my consciousness.

Late one afternoon we were taken to see one of the military hospitals near Guernica. The matron, who spoke perfect English, was the daughter of a famous Bilbao shipping family. She showed us first the up-to-date equipment of the hospital. Then we were taken to the wards, where we spoke to the men, all grievously wounded. As we were going out we passed a closed door at which I stopped. The matron said: "You will not want to go in there." "Why not?" I asked. She opened it and went in. I followed her. It was the morgue of the hospital. Covering the floor in long rows were dead soldiers. Concentrated there was the tragedy of Europe. The deathly stillness of that chamber was eloquent of the deep curse that hangs over the human adventure. The matron bent down and uncovered one of the faces. It lay calm and serene, beautiful with the unearthly beauty of death. No Franco could torment it any more. I remembered those beautiful words from the Apocrypha—"The souls of the righteous are in the hand of God; the care of them is with the most high . . . and no torment shall come nigh unto them." I turned my face away and the matron took my hand in both hers and said—"Yes, it is very sad, very sad, *but necessary*." Why necessary, I wondered? Can anything so tragically indicate human irrationality and sin as the necessity of violent slaughter? As we walked down the front steps, we met a young soldier, his head bloody, being helped up by an older man. The sight shocked me. People used to say of Dante as he walked the streets of Florence: "There goes a man who has been in hell." And I suddenly felt that I was beholding a man who had been in hell, too. Somehow the political issues were drowned in a flood of spiritual realization. "We are all in hell. We condemn one another to hell." I went to Spain convinced that nothing mattered except the defeat of Fascism. Face to face with that blood-stained soldier, I began to suspect that something else mattered even more than the defeat of Fascism.

I can present this as the symbol of what essentially, profoundly happened to me in Spain, happened, that is, in my deepest soul in the remote, inaccessible crevices of my being. I went to Spain a politician merely. I returned a theologian. Let the reader not mistake my meaning. In saying that I became a theologian, I do not lay any claim to theological learning or scholarship. In that sense I never have been nor ever shall be a theologian. What I mean is that the realization of an inner, personal need, beyond the power of social action to satisfy, displaced politics as the *supreme* issue in human existence. I might define theology as the science which deals with the fundamental personal need of the human being in all its variety of expression.

So in Spain I became theological, which means that I was committed to a revaluation of all my political interests and judgments—a long process. It was in Spain that the necessity for this came into being. Social development and historic progress ceased to be the supreme end and value. Now it began to appear as an element in the drama of the personal soul.

We experienced great difficulty in getting away from Bilbao. First, we were taken to Santander. There we hung about for six hours to no purpose, but made the acquaintance of a delightful young officer who informed us that he was studying English literature. He fetched us the book he was reading, which turned out to be Samuel Smiles' *Self-Help!* I roared! A young republican revolutionary studying that supreme capitalist classic! He was most kind. At regular intervals he served us with enormous mugs of tea, which I relished. Our second attempt to get away (by air) was frustrated by bad weather. In Bilbao it was lovely, but at Toulouse there was snow! Finally we got away in a French destroyer from Bermeo. It landed us in St. Jean de Luz. The same night the Dean left for Madrid. Macmurray and I entrained for Paris, and a more delightful companion than he one could not desire. I hope we shall be in the same boat when we cross the Styx.

I stayed in Paris to address a meeting of French Catholics, at which I had the pleasure of meeting George Bernanos, author of *The Diary of a Country Priest*. Together with Maritain, he was making a brave effort to stem the tide of French Catholic reaction on Spain. Alas! to no purpose. Republican Spain slowly bled to death, and the churches—Protestant as well as Catholic—looked on with folded arms. Wilson Steer, who was staying at the same hotel in Bilbao, was sure that England and France were in for a terrible retribution.

2

Returning to London, I entered on the work of Spanish propaganda, but with an increasingly divided mind and ebbing energy. The inner stress was becoming intolerable. In the final conflict of the soul, when the need for release from the burden and death of existence has become overwhelming, not even issues of world importance can enable the soul to stand the strain. When the spirit has reached breaking point, historic issues are powerless. When a man has touched rock-bottom and cries out, "Oh wretched man that I am! Who shall deliver me?" even the greatest of social problems loses its significance—until that primary personal cry is answered. If existence is itself dust and ashes, what do Fascism, Communism, Socialism, New Orders, matter? That was the point I had reached. I had entered the valley of Achor. I was in the throes of the final anguish. I was dying my second death before my first.

It is an amazing thing that a man can fight Armageddon in his deep, inner being without an echo of it reaching the society in which he lives and works. Down in that Cimmerian region the heaviest guns fire, and the heaviest bombs explode without the faintest sound coming to the ears of people round about. A cosmic, super-historic citadel can be overthrown in the inner depths, with a force that makes angels and spirits tremble, with an explosiveness which reaches heaven in a reverberating rumbling, without the slightest disturbance in the immediate environment. None suspected in the meetings I now addressed, for example, that the speaker was enduring the final agony. One made one's points and uttered one's appeal without a sign.

The process went on for some months. I carried on as long as I could. I felt that I must do the job that lay nearest. It is a good rule. When one's world is falling about one's ears, and one's whole scheme of life is disintegrating to bits, cling to the obvious duty . . . I went to all parts of the country to speak on behalf of the Spanish people. But it was a ghastly business. I felt like the man in that terrible story of Edgar Allan Poe, who was imprisoned in a torture chamber, the ceiling of which was relentlessly descending in fractions of inches. At long last, it would crush him like a beetle. I could not just sit still and watch my descending fate. I had to do something—and I did the one remaining thing that I felt as an obligation.

I set out to raise funds to despatch a food-ship to Bilbao. The delegation, on its return, had undertaken to send out a cargo of food, which it succeeded in doing, though late. We organized a public meeting at the Friends' Meeting House, Euston Road, which was addressed by the Dean, Macmurray and myself. A few members of the delegation (which had now been transformed into a Committee) had the jitters about that meeting; but it was a great success. I felt, in spite of everything, that I had never spoken better in all my life. The large hall was packed to capacity. I believe, even though I were dying, that a great audience would galvanize me into energetic life. It fell to my lot to make the appeal for funds. We did not make an ordinary collection. We asked for offerings. I followed the practice first introduced by Isobel Brown at Communist meetings of asking for contributions of big sums, then for smaller sums and so down to passing round the plate. I started by asking for £50—and we got it! Miss Maude Royden sent up a cheque to the platform. I believe we raised nearly £400 at that meeting. At one bound, I had become an expert money extractor. Why not? Hadn't I been a parson for ten years?

On behalf of the committee, I addressed meetings in Manchester, North Wales and the West of England. Some of the churches in North Wales responded generously. I had a great time, I remember, among the quarrymen in Caernarvonshire. During June and July I was away three or four nights a week, doing speaking tours. As I look back, I feel some satisfaction for the work I did in connection with Spain. I did what lay in my power to awaken my fellow-countrymen to the great need of the people, to the significance of their struggle and to its peril for Europe. But on the England of 1935-9, there was a blight. It lay on the whole nation.

In the course of my Spanish work it was my privilege to

meet many good and great people. Most of them were
obscure, unknown folk. In history they are nameless, but
not in the book of life. There they are recorded in letters of
the purest flame, miners, quarrymen, railwaymen, clerks,
who gave their lives so that freedom should not perish from
the earth. They are buried in Spanish soil. So there are bits
of pain that are for ever England, the England of the
Puritans, of the Lollards, of the Tolpuddle Martyrs, of the
Chartists; the England that humbled the royal tyrant, that
withstood Napoleon, that defended against Hitler the last
bastion of liberty against a fouler tyranny than the planet
has ever known. Let us praise God for the heroism, for the
sacrifice of the world's nameless children, even though they
know Him not yet. They died for freedom—a great thing
for which to die. I also met and worked with scores of ordinary, decent, sinful men and women who lived for liberty.
After a long day at a London desk or factory, or warehouse,
they gave all their leisure to writing letters, keeping index-
cards, stewarding meetings and a hundred other tasks, so
that Fascism should "not pass". They gave not only their
time, but also their hard-earned pennies and shillings. They
showed superlative devotion. Liberty is indeed a powerful
magnet, and it must be so; for God has made man free.
Tyrants who seek to enslave men are trying to undo God's
work. Against them, a deep instinct moves clerks, shop-
assistants, street-sweepers and the nameless multitudes of
all tribes and peoples and races to a deathless resistance.

Of the prominent people that I met, none impressed me
more than Wilfred Steer, *The Times* correspondent, and the
Duchess of Atholl. Journalists of the "foreign correspondent" class are a distinct race, of whom America and Britain have thrown up magnificent examples in the troubled
years of our recent past. Think of John Gunther, Gedye,
Douglas Reed, Edgar Mowrer, W. H. Chamberlin, Eugene
Lyons and many many more. What is it that distinguishes
them? I think it is their courage, their passion for truth,

their blazing hatred of barbarism and cruelty. On my last morning in Bilbao, when I was awakened early by the air-raid warning, I threw on my dressing-gown and went down-stairs. There I met Steer in his pyjamas, on his way out. I followed him as also did the Dean, an ecclesiastical dignitary in undress. The raiders were overhead and shells were burst-ing. Steer was as unconcerned as could be. "Those are Italians," he said. I wondered how he could tell. "By the height at which they are flying," he said; "the German will risk coming down, but not the Italian." He was modest, objective, and clear-eyed in his estimate of things. I should say that, on the whole, the foreign correspondent is the least egotistic and vain of all the professions. Certainly much less than actors, artists or preachers. In this Steer was true to type. He came to Spain from Abyssinia, but he did not obtrude the fact.

The Duchess of Atholl I came to know fairly well. The more I got to know her, the more highly I thought of her. A remarkable woman, not afraid to challenge fate or for-tune, who threw herself whole-heartedly into the Spanish struggle. She completely transcended the outlook of her class. She showed a clear grasp of the meaning of Nazism. What impressed me most was her unaffected simplicity, her high-mindedness, her sense of public duty. Her defeat at a by-election was a great misfortune. She was of greater moral worth to British politics than the whole of the Front Bench put together and was one of the most distinguished casualties in the Spanish Civil War.

In the August of 1937, I went with my wife and little girl for a holiday to Southerndown, on the Glamorgan coast. I had come to the end of my tether. By August, Spain and every other public issue were drowned in the flood of per-sonal despair.

CHAPTER XII

DE PROFUNDIS CLAMAVI

IT IS INTERESTING, at least, to observe that, in a state of great psychic stress, the memory seems to function automatically. It is a curious fact. One would assume that when one is most distressed by inner personal conflict and despair, external happenings would be forgotten. Yet, in my experience, the opposite is the truth. The external details of that holiday, from the journey out to the return home, are impressed on my mind with the clearness of an etching. I remember, for instance, how tormenting was my little girl, then only a year and a half old, on the journey from Paddington to Bridgend. It is, I am sure, the earnest wish of every parent travelling with a young child that it will go to sleep on the journey. On this occasion, Diana refused to oblige. I took turns with my wife to entertain her, walking her up and down the corridor, but it was a terrible journey.

I

Southerndown was associated in my mind with boyhood experiences, with adolescence and the threshold of life. Mixed with early hopes and ambitions. When a youth working in the colliery in Maesteg, only fourteen miles away, I frequently went to Southerndown on Saturday afternoons in summer. Walking along the cliffs, I committed my dreams of future achievement to the winds and waves. After I had been admitted to United College, Bradford, I went to Southerndown for a day, happy and exalted. This visit in 1937 was the first since then. What a contrast! Then full of hope, vitality, enthusiasm and faith; now, twenty-five years later, bereft of faith, and in deep despair. After a generation of intense experience, the fires of belief and faith had been reduced to ashes. The dreams I had flung to the waves were coming back in mocking echoes.

I have described here, as truthfully as I have been able, the collapse of my working faith, of my religion, which ended in the dissipation of my political and social idealism. By August, 1937, all the great public issues of our time had, for me, been emptied of their meaning. From that disaster I had nothing on which to fall back. My personal and domestic environment were even a more desolate wilderness. Step by step, my personal relationships had disintegrated with my public activity. My marriage had broken down. The only tie that bound my wife and me, which merely preserved the outer framework, was our little daughter. Love and its spirit had fled.

In this too I have drunk to the full my generation's cup of bitterness and disillusion. In no relationship in our world has there been such disintegration and failure as in that of sex and marriage. Against human omnipotence, against the delusion of human sovereignty, no sanctity is safe. Marriage is one of the final sanctities of European society. We have lived to see it invaded by the seven devils of secularity. I doubt whether anyone can really enter into the spirit of the typically modern man who has not had some experience, in one form or another, of sexual disharmony and failure. My experience of it went very far.

It is indeed a melancholy tragedy to see love slipping away and to feel utterly powerless to do anything to prevent it. When we first met I fell head over heels in love with my wife, as she with me. Our marriage was the fruit of romantic ecstasy. Such love, one thinks, could never fade. Alas! it did. In truth, very soon after we were married, we drifted apart. The birth of our little girl momentarily arrested the drift, but only momentarily. The deep current of disunion in mind and heart carried us further and further away from each other. Only the fact of Diana kept us outwardly

together. It was she, and she alone, that prevented the final
severance.

I must emphasize that I had tried to will it otherwise. We
both made efforts, from time to time, to recover our lost
love, but to no purpose. The spirit had fled, and we tor-
mented even when we intended to help each other. The fact
that we had common interests did not solve our problem.
My wife entered fully into my People's Front work, and
still more into Spanish Aid. She did a great deal of the
secretarial work of the propaganda committee. I proved to
the full that common public interests alone cannot make two
people happy in the marriage bond.

My whole life was by this time in ruins. That was the
grim and simple fact. Most of the holiday I spent alone with
my own sombre communings. The first part of the morning I accompanied my wife and child to the beach. Diana
loved the sea. I looked after her while my wife had her
morning swim. I then walked off and sat for hours on the
rocks, numbed with fruitless thoughts and blank despair.
In the evenings, I set off for long tramps alone.

One gets to a point at which pain becomes too deep to be
felt, and one passes over into mental coma. At that point I
had now arrived. Consciously, I lived in the immediate
present, but unconsciously, I was being carried beyond my
will. Thought ceased. I merely noted my sensations. I saw
seagulls in swooping flight, and said to myself: "That bird
is coming down to the water." Or I watched the tide flow-
ing in and wondered whether the incoming wave would
reach farther than the last. My conscious mind let go the
burden of despair. It handed it over to the unconscious, and
contented itself with reacting to the succession of sense-
impressions. But deep down, strange decisions were being
shaped beyond my knowledge and participation. Outwardly I lived in the passing moment and for the passing
moment. I was in a condition of utter indifference to anything beyond what my five senses could grasp. Without

knowing it at the time, I was doing what the Psalmist commanded: "Be still and know that I am God," which my friend Professor Vernon Lewis of Brecon translated—"Just let go and you will discover who God is."

2

One evening, after supper, I set off in the pouring rain. I took a circular path over fields which ultimately brought me back to my starting-point. From a cloud-laden sky, the rain beat fiercely on to my face, and I felt some kind of savage joy and satisfaction. I suddenly said to myself: "Why don't you end it all?" The despair which my conscious mind had transferred to my unconscious mind had at last taken shape in the decision to commit suicide. "Why not end it all?" Why not indeed! As I faced that grim question I recovered vitality. There surged through my being an ecstasy, an exaltation. A suddenly realized will-to-die galvanized me into new energy. Rain and wind answered to the storm within, with terrific, explosive certainty. The thought of returning to London to resume the old round of meetings, committees, domestic strain and the hundred other things became loathsome. No! Never! I clung to that one purpose that I should make an end of it here in Southerndown.

I realized that I was standing with the beach below. It was late. The night was dark, I could hear the waves beating up against the rocks. In a strange excitement I made my way down to the sea, sat on a rock and gazed round. Behind me was a light in a window, and I found myself wondering, as though it did not concern me, whether it was our bungalow. Then I looked out to sea. It was all dark except for the white foam of the waters. Before I realized it, the waves had reached where I sat. Swept by an eerie emotional exaltation, I plunged into the dark waters.

I must have swum, though I am a poor swimmer. Then

in a flash, a thunderous flash, I realized what I was doing. "Good God! What am I doing?" With despairing strength, I swam back. Oh that struggle! I was suspended between life and death!

I felt my feet touch bottom and waded out, out beyond the reach of the tide. I sat down and broke into a convulsion of weeping. Suddenly, unaccountably, there came to my mind—so vividly—a picture of my mother teaching me the catechism from the little book, *Rhodd Mam* (My Mother's Gift). It was so powerful and clear. I saw the kitchen and the armchair in which my mother sat. I saw the spectacles half-way down her nose. I saw the little iron stand on which I sat beside her. And I heard her saying—"Who is Jesus Christ?" to which I answered, "Jesus Christ is my Saviour". It was just like that. A deep peace, literally "the peace which the world can neither give nor take away", flooded my entire being. I knew I had passed through the great tribulation. "Rock of Ages—cleft for *me*—naked come to Thee for dress." In the final anguish, hovering between life and death, I found myself, as I was, and in my utter nakedness and worthlessness I found God. And finding Him, though this was not realized until later, I found everything. How had it happened? Who can tell? "The wind bloweth where it listeth and thou hearest the sound thereof, but canst not tell whence it cometh nor whither it goeth."

It was in deepest despair that I came face to face with God. Is it at all surprising, then, that I look upon despair as a necessary element in the Christian experience? I had but repeated the classic Christian discovery in all ages. What did St. Paul mean by his dark cry, "Oh wretched man that I am!"? What had Augustine suffered before light came to him? What was the condition of Francis of Assisi when he ceased to be the young man about town? That marvellous gaiety of his later life was rooted in dark despair. Through what had Kierkegaard passed before he came to certainty? My own experience confirmed so wonderfully the truth of the Bible, and the comprehension of the Church, that no man or woman can pass from death to life, without first realizing utter self-despair. No one can find God as Redeemer who still flirts with the possibility that one can redeem oneself. That final pride in one's own power must be irremediably broken. This is the rock of stumbling, the great offence of the Cross to the mind of fallen man, especially the fallen mind of modern man. To admit our powerlessness, not as a bloodless intellectual thesis, but as a desperate, ontological destruction. That is to uproot man from his dearest delusion. It will take more than two world wars to do that, even such a world war of bestiality and horror as the one through which we had still to go. "Ye must be born again." Absolutely! There are many things on which the Church can afford to compromise; but this necessity for abandonment of self-pride and self-power before man can find redemption is not one of them. Away with the pernicious, disastrous lie of the naturally Christian mind, the *anima Christiana naturaliter*! Every human soul born into this world must be reborn. "Except a man be born again, he cannot see the Kingdom of God."

People frequently ask me if it is necessary for everyone to pass through such an experience as that which I suffered, before realizing Christian certainty. To which I reply that the form of the experience is immaterial, but its substance, its essence, is utterly necessary. You must come to the realization of your own complete powerlessness. Now, with the best will in the world, I find it very difficult to imagine how such a realization, whatever its form, can be an imperceptible process. It is a transition from death to life! There is nothing natural in that. It is super-natural. It is unnatural. In Nature, the organism does not come back to life after it has died. Its death may be another's life, but never a renewal of its own life. To die in oneself and to live again another life is anti-natural. How can that happen without some sort of conflict and anguish? It is like a revolution in the State. Could power pass from one class to another without citizens being aware of it? Hardly! How much less can the soul of man be unaware of its transition from the old humanity to the new!

I suspect that this question is itself a disguised attempt to escape the final necessity of the new birth; a rationalization of the unwillingness to let go of ourselves. That is one of the results—and the worst—of modernist Christianity. I am not unmindful of the great services which Modernism has rendered to the Church; far from it. But my appreciation of these services of scholarship and social emphasis does not blind me to its disastrous error and disservice, its vulgarization of the revolutionary new birth into a mere natural, psychological process. A generation which has been poisoned by this ghastly heresy finds it very, very difficult to realize the necessity of a revolutionary second birth for every human soul, and especially for themselves.

3

It would be very romantic if I could say that from that moment on the Southerndown beach, all was clear and straightforward and ecstatic. It would not be true. For some time I was a convalescent slowly coming back to strength from the edge of the grave. Despair had gone. I knew and felt that I had begun life anew. On my return to London, I was a different man. The man I was had ceased to be. In Christ I had become a new creation.

When I got back to London, I remembered Niebuhr and his book, *Reflections on the End of Era*. I re-read it and my mind was flooded with light. I got hold of his other books, and laid hands on everything he had written. First I devoured—that is the right word!—his *Does Modern Civilization Need Religion?* Afterwards followed *Moral Man and Immoral Society*, and *Leaves from the Notebook of a Tamed Cynic*. Niebuhr formulated for me in sharp outline the thing which I had experienced myself—the fatality of radical sin. He drew from it the bold conclusion that this fact of sin made it impossible for man ever to achieve Utopia, but at the same time made the historic effort towards Utopia a thing of eternal significance. I can never be sufficiently grateful to Reinhold Niebuhr for what his books did for me. He fitted together the elements of my last ten years' experience. The more of him that I read the more clearly I came to see, not only the meaning of my own experience, but the meaning of European politics and indeed of European history. But something happened even better than this. I fell in love anew with my wife and our marriage was re-made. There happened, that is to say, what the moderns said was impossible. Once love has gone, say the moderns, it is impossible to re-create it. A marriage once broken cannot be repaired. That is not true. I found myself caring for my wife in a new way. And whilst we would not qualify for the Dunmow Flitch—and I hope we never shall—we remained happy together. Together we have come through the great tribulation to live a significant life of truth and comradeship. Much mutual forgiveness has brought a great mutual love and tolerance and understanding.

From the reading of Niebuhr, I went to the Bible. I drenched myself in the Bible, more particularly in the prophets, Psalms, St. John, the Epistles and Revelation. The Bible spoke to me as never before. No commentary on it is so illuminating as the sharing of its experience. I felt I knew exactly what Paul meant by the seventh chapter of Romans; what Jeremiah meant when he said that the heart of man was deceitful and desperately sick; what Peter felt when he cried out that he was a sinful man. I confess that I cannot help feeling how trivial is the method of trying to prove that Original Sin is Biblical by quoting texts. When Modernists ask me to *prove* the doctrine of Original Sin in the Bible, I just marvel. How can one read the Bible at all without sensing that it is a world of tragedy, of utter human calamity and impotence, and of a Divine redemption? If a man must have texts, even critically used, to convince him that the Bible is a literature of radical sin—well, the texts will not convince. No text will convince the typical non-Christian humanist. A very gifted contemporary writer, for example, can see in the historical portions of the Old Testament nothing but a tale of sheiks. What can one do in the face of such blindness?

I must not retrace the ground I have already traversed in *On To Orthodoxy*, where I afterwards described at length the theological process of the new significance of life in terms of events. In a very real sense, everything became new for me. My home life became vastly different, and, indeed, everything was different.

I felt now greatly the need for worship. So I began to attend church once again. I went fairly regularly for a while to Lyndhurst Road Congregational Church, where Dr. John Short ministered. But I roamed a bit. Occasionally I went to Westminster Chapel to hear Dr. Martin Lloyd-Jones, whose influence on me defies analysis. He was not a thinker; he had no background of theological culture; he had no literary gift. Yet he held me. Something in the man spoke to the deeps in me.

By some chance or other, which I have not forgotten, I renewed contact with one I had met in the Mitrinović days, Malcolm Spencer, secretary of the Social Service Committee of the Congregational Union, one of the few Christians in the world, a very true and gracious friend, with a delicious sense of humour. He was the worst-dressed parson I have known, worse even than myself. It seems that on one occasion, when new missionaries were being presented at the May Meetings of the Congregational Union in the City Temple, the dress of a few of them was somewhat Bohemian. Some wore flannels and sports coats and some of the women were hatless and stockingless. This was seriously criticized at a committee meeting, and threatened to assume serious proportions. By a happy stroke, the chairman moved that the whole matter of candidates' garb should be referred to—Malcolm Spencer! Nobody enjoyed the joke more than he.

Malcolm invited me to co-operate in the work of a Christian Social Council Committee on finance and industry, which I did. I found it rather fruitless, for the council was deeply poisoned by Social Credit. Demant was its Research Secretary. This committee, whilst not committed to Douglas, was dominated by the idea that finance was the only thing wrong with Capitalism. With my Marxist training, I could not endure any such nonsense, so I was always up against the others and I inevitably impeded progress. If Malcolm ever felt any impatience, he never showed it, except to administer a sly dig at me now and again.

We became very friendly. He suggested that I should go to the Rhondda valley to make an investigation into the effect of the economic depression on the life of the churches, which would mean that I should have to take a temporary pastorate at the English Congregational Church at Tonypandy. It appealed to me very much. To be back in the ministry again, if even only for one month! I went to the Rhondda for the month of April, 1938. It was a wonderful experience. It was a joy to preach once again. This time I had a Gospel, *the* Gospel, the Gospel "once for all delivered unto the saints".

Except for one thing, that experience was an unalloyed happiness. The one exception was the burden of public prayer. I dreaded the prospect of having to make four public prayers each Sunday. I began to feel the need of a liturgical service. What idiocy, I came to feel, not to draw upon the experience of the saints of Christendom! Soon, that need became imperative for me. Extempore prayer, when feelingly and fittingly offered, is beautiful, but, below its best, it can be dreadful. A liturgy can become lifeless and mechanical, but I find even that preferable to the garrulity and vulgarity of much extempore prayer. I dreaded becoming glib.

I made my report to the Social Service Committee of the Congregational Union, which, I gathered, rather upset one or two members of the committee. Some of the things I said about unemployment were thought to be extreme. Malcolm, who verifies all his references, even the one after the last, submitted my report to one of the South Wales ministers who was familiar with the whole problem. He thought it a good report, except that I had understated the effect of unemployment!

My month's work in Tonypandy had accentuated a desire to return to the ministry. I became profoundly certain of a "call" back to the pulpit. With this in view I went to see Dr. Sidney Berry. He gave me a very warm and friendly reception and encouraged me to hope that I should return to the Congregational pulpit. There were difficulties, certainly. My record in Southport was not good. Official Congregationalism, like officialdom everywhere, looks askance at the disturber of the institution. Still, Dr. Berry was kind enough to say that my voice was needed in Congregationalism, though, he said, there were not many churches to which I could minister. Apparently, I was too intellectual!

Congregationalism lives on its preaching. Without great preaching it will die. It is my impression—not my opinion or considered belief, but merely impression—that Congregationalism is slowly dying. It is an impression shared by some of the ablest men in Congregationalism today.

After my return from Tonypandy, nothing was done. But I was determined to preach. I joined the fellowship of the Church at Highbury Quadrant, where an old fellow-student, the Rev. Ralph Turner, was minister. Meanwhile, something else happened, which opened the way back to the ministry.

CHAPTER XIII

"HE AROSE AND WENT TO HIS FATHER"

AMONGST MANY ACTIVITIES in London had been lecture engagements with the Hampstead Ethical Society, the secretary of which, Alex Dawn, and his brother, Sydney, were great personal friends. At least once, and sometimes twice, each session, I lectured. As usual, I was asked to give a date in the winter of 1938. When I informed Alex that I had become an orthodox Christian, and could not lecture to the Society any more, he replied with fine tolerance, "Why not?" "The society," I said, "will not want to listen to a confession of faith from me." "If it is your faith," he replied, "it will be worth hearing." So I decided to lecture on "Does Modern Civilization Need Religion?"

I endeavoured to show the curse of Original Sin and the need for release from it, which society was powerless to effect. It provoked a lively, but good-tempered discussion. Nobody agreed with me. On my way home I suddenly decided that I would write a book on the subject. I told my wife: "I am going to write a book." "What about?" she asked. "Original Sin!" I was so excited that after a bite of supper, I set off for a long tramp over Hampstead Heath, in the course of which the book was conceived and took shape. But instead of being a thesis on Original Sin, it became instead a record of my rediscovery of religion. I gave it the title "A Modernist's Rediscovery of Orthodoxy".

The book took possession of me. I rested neither day nor night. I was driven to write by an inner compulsion. I did not stay to wonder whether it would be published. I am sure that I was sceptical, for I had already written one book of about 130,000 words, which had been refused by two publishers. It would be true to say that I wrote my book for my own satisfaction.

The writing took me about five weeks, one sustained effort. I read it through. It is the habit of authors to say that they are never satisfied with their work. I frankly confess that I was more than satisfied. I had occasion to see Dr. Sidney Berry and told him that I had written the book, which, I said, had a touch of greatness in it. He roared with laughter.

Round about this time, I had the pleasure of meeting Dr. Martin Lloyd-Jones. I had written an article under the title *De Profundis Clamavi*: "The disillusionment of a Rationalist." He suggested I should send it to the *British Weekly*. I told him that I had now completed a book, and he put me in touch with Hodder and Stoughton. In due course, they accepted it. Mr. Paul Hodder-Williams wanted a different title. "A Modernist's Rediscovery of Orthodoxy" was clumsy. "What about Back to Orthodoxy"? *Back* to Orthodoxy missed the whole point. I said "*On* to Orthodoxy". and that was how the title came.

Meanwhile Malcolm Spencer informed me that he had been given a cheque to use at his own discretion, and he proposed that I should go back to Rhondda for three months. Malcolm knew how eager and determined I was to return to the ministry. He was doing everything in his power to prepare the way for me. He got me into touch with the South Wales Moderator, the Rev. Gwilym Rees, who was then and later kind and encouraging, and it was fixed that I should return to Tonypandy for three months from August to October.

In September, 1939, my book was published. In view of the outbreak of war, I was very dubious about its fate. I expected it to be still-born. On the contrary, it surpassed all expectations, and received a really wonderful press. Out of nearly forty reviews, only one was unfavourable, by Dr. Selbie in the *Congregational Quarterly*, which provoked very

many angry letters of protest from prominent Congregationalists. But I could not really complain, for on the whole
my own denomination welcomed the book. The one
criticism was that it was not orthodox enough!

On To Orthodoxy brought me hundreds of letters from all
over the world. One of the most moving was from a missionary in Africa who said it had given him new life. He
was on the point of resigning, as he felt at the end of his
tether; my book had made things new for him. That letter
gave me a great joy. The book also brought me many new
friends. I spent a very happy week-end with the Principal
of Mansfield College, Oxford, and on that occasion I
preached at St. Mary's, Oxford. I got an immense thrill as
I realized I was preaching in Newman's old pulpit. I can
probably claim to have preached from two pulpits, one
where Newman preached and the other where Lenin spoke.

I also spent a happy time with Dr. Whale and his students
at Cheshunt, when I preached in the chapel, where I was a
little ill-at-ease, because I spoke from the manuscript for
the first time for many years. After dinner Dr. Whale told
the men they could take me to their studies and stay up
all night if they wanted to. We nearly did. I was as happy as
a sandboy. I made Dr. Whale green with envy when I told
him that my average sleep was four to five hours a night!

Nothing gave me greater pleasure than the renewal of my
friendship with Professor Bertram Woolf, of New College,
London. We were good friends in my Southport days, when
he was in Liverpool. He was a man of solid, weighty
scholarship. I tread softly in his presence. The book earned
me the friendship of Professor Vernon Lewis of Brecon, too
little known in England, one of the most significant figures
in Welsh religious life. Twenty years before this he had
translated Barth into Welsh.

I was inundated with invitations to preach, lecture and
write. So the problem of my return to the ministry was
ended and I was settled at Richmond Road Congregational

Church, Cardiff. I started my ministry in December, 1939, and it was agreed I should stay one year. In February, I was formally inducted to the pastorate by Dr. Whale, who, altogether delightful and charming, a man who had strayed from the seventeenth to the twentieth century, spoke of things which his generation did not want to hear—sin and hell, repentance and faith, death and redemption.

I

So there I was back in the regular ministry after twelve years in the wilderness. My first ministerial period started during the first world war; my second during the second. Now I had a first-hand experience of the power of Christ, a first-hand knowledge of God. For that experience I had had to pay a great price in terms of human frustration, defeat and suffering. But the pearl was mine. Now I had a faith that could stand up to any disaster time could bring. I was able to do the one essential of the ministerial calling, namely, to witness to the redeeming power of Jesus Christ. Now I felt I could take my place on the witness-stand and say: "Yes! This is true: Christ can and does save men from despair and doom. He has done it to me." Amid all the complexity and confusion of our time, I am forever sure of the redeeming power of God in Christ. Though all the world were to unite in denying this, I should still be certain. This one thing I know, whereas I was blind, now I see. "From dark despair He plucked me." I could witness to this as something that had happened, an event in time and place. This certainty was the core of everything I had to say. This was the supreme, comprehensive difference between my new ministry and the old. From it flowed profound and revolutionary differences in preaching.

I noted great differences in the Congregational Church to which I belonged. There was a colder spiritual climate. To a much greater extent than in previous years, there was greater strangeness to fundamental Christian experience. This was reflected in the preaching. The deepest and most significant preachers were, it seemed to me, the least popular.

This fact was also reflected in the kind of problems that occupied the attention of the denomination. They were predominantly economic, such as the increasing financial difficulty experienced by the churches, especially in the support of the ministry; the grave decline in the support of the missionary task, and so forth. I did not know the statistics, but I was fairly confident that there were a greater number of vacant pastorates than ever before. Churches were increasingly reluctant to give calls to men, because of the financial strain in meeting their salaries. Like the most secular of institutions, the Church is subject to the pressure of a declining capitalism. I realized that the predominance of these problems indicated grave decline in the spiritual reality of Christian experience. When religious organizations are obsessed with the question how to find money, it is a sure sign of spiritual decay.

The spiritual decline is no less reflected in the decline of congregations. There was a decreasing sense of the need for worship. Nothing was so symptomatic of the secularization of the Church as this fact. I was especially struck by this decline of worship in the changes I observed in Welsh religious life after an interval of about twenty-seven years. A generation ago, it was a general rule in Welsh Independency that the congregations were larger than the membership. I found that no longer so. They were invariably smaller. Cardiff, for instance, had two or three famous Independent Churches: all their evening congregations were very much smaller than their membership. And I was assured that this condition obtained throughout South Wales. It was certainly true of churches I knew as a youth, whose Sunday evening congregations were but a shadow of their former ones. The week-night prayer-meeting, once a great factor in Welsh religious life, had degenerated into a comparative nullity. The Church was wading in the shallows.

I was struck no less with the decline in the calibre of the ministry. It is always a temptation to say that today is not as good as yesterday. But I thought that the intellectual and spiritual quality of the ministry was lower than that of the generation before. Economic causes, I am sure, have played their part. The average ministerial salary in South Wales was wretched. Economic causes, too, were compelling ministers to spend more and more time in augmenting their salaries. The effect of this on intellectual discipline was disastrous.

Yet the situation the minster had to face then and faces today makes much greater spiritual and intellectual demands than upon his predecessors of generations ago. But he seemed less equipped to meet them. In a disintegrating society, as ours certainly is, politics and economics play a much greater part than in a stabilized, progressive society. They become elements of the first importance in the problem of the philosophy of history. A prophetic Christianity always speaks in terms of a philosophy of history. And Christianity becomes uniquely prophetic in eras of social collapse. In an age of power politics which existed then and is still maintained, how can ministers speak the word of historic judgment without a thorough knowledge of politics, history and economics? The situation is making heavy intellectual demands upon ministers. Are they adequately meeting them? They were not when I returned, and I hesitate to answer "yes" even now.

Yet in this gloomy situation, there is one fact of hope, as I see it. I was invited by the East Glamorgan Congregational Association to address its Quarterly Meetings in October, 1939, when I spoke on the Christian Faith in the Modern World. Very bluntly I argued that the modern situation was symptomatic of the collapse of Humanism, and its religious parallel, Modernism. Christianity faces this situation with its assertion of the root sin of man, of his impotence to overcome it, and of his consequent need of a Saviour, none other than Jesus Christ. In the ensuing discussion, all the younger ministers supported my position. Its opponents were old men.

This tendency for younger men to turn away from Modernism to a new orthodoxy is, I believe, a symptom of hope. It heralds the end of a whole era, during which the Church tended to pin its faith to the recuperative, redemptive power of man. This delusion vanished in the horrors of the second world war. There is now, I think, the promise in the young men's "theological repentance" of a new era in which the Church will realize that man is something to be transcended, first by being broken, and then re-made, nearer to the desire of God.

2

I found my work at Cardiff of absorbing interest, both preaching and writing, for which I enjoyed ever widening opportunity. I thought of myself first and foremost as a preacher; for God had called me to preach. When my wife was filling my registration papers, she asked: "How shall I describe your occupation, minister or author?" I replied —"Minister!" In all my public utterances whether in the pulpit or on the platform, I felt and feel I am preaching. I found, however, that conditions in the Congregational pastorate to be such that it was impossible to combine what was demanded of me with serious study and research. The minister was half strangled with the demands of organization and every man had to be a general practitioner. That is one of its weaknesses. But I was determined not to give up my writing and study. I soon realized that I had to accept one or two alternatives: to surrender all thought of serious, original work, or to continue my writing and give up the pastorate. Unless I was lucky enough to get a church which would be content to expect only preaching and the necessary pastoral visitation—and nothing more. This dilemma I put to Dr. J. D. Jones. He frankly doubted whether there was such a church left in Congregationalism. That opened my eyes. Gwilym Rees, the Moderator of Wales and Monmouth, said the same thing. So did others. I told Dr. Berry, in his room at Memorial Hall, what I had in mind, and suggested that I might be found a country pastorate, where I should be expected only to preach and visit, so as to have time to write. He laughed his hearty laugh and said, "My dear boy, you should go to the Church of England. We have no such churches." I got the impression he was joking and thought no more of it.

If Congregationalism has no such churches, or at best only a few, it was quite certain that my chances to minister to one of them were meagre. A prodigal son had no right to expect one of the "plums". Congregationalism does not kill the fatted calf for prodigal sons.

When I decided to seek Orders in the Church of England I informed Dr. Berry of my decision, he wished me well. "I am no denominationalist, D.R., as you know. God bless you. I hope you will be happy." Those were his words. And I shall be grateful to him for ever.

CHAPTER XIV

FINDING MYSELF

THE STEP I now took was the final realization of my own self-discovery. One day when preaching at Bournemouth I met Bishop Walter Carey. He talked to me about the Church of England. I cannot say that my mind was perceptibly turning in that direction, for while I had been thinking vaguely of the Methodist Church, also of the Presbyterian Church of England as possible future spheres of work, I certainly had no idea of the Anglican Church. But the Bishop deeply interested me. I was convinced of the breakdown of Congregational church polity and the need for liturgical support in the ministry I sought to give, and Bishop Carey, with insight and great intelligence, yet without any obvious persuasive effect, enabled me to realize what the English Church had to offer to meet my need. I told him that I was not without sincere appreciation of the merits and historical greatness of Independency, but had become convinced that it had outlived its time, and that corporate association in Church order was necessary for sustained Christian life. The Bishop had read *On To Orthodoxy*, and on his advice I wrote Archbishop Temple a long letter in which I gave an outline of my problem.

The Archbishop had also read the book and welcomed my letter. After a talk, he strongly advised me to pay a visit to St. Deiniol's Library, Hawarden, North Wales, to become acquainted with the Rev. Alec Vidler, its warden. This I did.

Early in June, 1940, I went to St. Deiniol's Library to meet Mr. Vidler, and at the very first Matins at the little chapel I knew that I had come home. I had not attended an Anglican service before. I was fifty years old. I was not a raw youth to be impressed. I came with a lifetime of suffering, and found that "I was in the spirit", deep called to deep. Late that first night I sat up reading, for the first time in my life, *The Book of Common Prayer*. "How is it", I asked myself, "that I have never read this before?" I found the Prayer Book to be more exciting at that first reading than any novel. I experienced a sense of ecstasy, I knew that I had found my spiritual place of abiding, that my buffeted, storm-tossed barque had reached its haven.

I discussed the possibility of embarking on a course of study at the library and after the Archbishop had with characteristic generosity lent me some money (for I had nothing) to enable me to leave my wife and child provided for, I went back there in October, 1940, to stay for six months.

During that time I was confirmed. It was a blessed time, for I was given the opportunity to absorb the tradition and ethos of the Church of England. I kept many a tryst in the chapel with the Lord. I had entered into a new inheritance. Every day I was finding new treasures. I recall the thrilling wonder with which I heard the Collect on Advent Sunday in the parish church of Hawarden. And every day I was seeing deeper and deeper into the Daily Offices of Matins and Evensong.

The General Confession so excited and moved me that I wrote a book about it during these months, which was later published under the title *Down Peacock's Feathers*. It was Alec Vidler who found the title for me in one of the Homilies. For that, and for so much more, too near to me to be able to recount it, I owe him inexpressible thanks. He was a Father in God to me, so full of insight, so full of Spirit, and yet so human in his understanding, that my stay in the Library became a holy and yet a richly enjoyable time. At the end I was accepted as a candidate for Holy Orders, Alec writing to the Archbishop that he had never had one who believed more whole-heartedly in the Thirty-nine Articles than I!

So I was ordained deacon, in Lent, 1941, by William Temple, then Archbishop of York, in York Minster. What a wonderful place in which to receive my commission! I could hardly contain the joy that surged within my heart and soul. The following Trinity, also in York Minster, I was given my priest's orders. I had found my way into the Church of England because God had led me there.

While at Hawarden, I broadcast on the radio quite often, and particularly enjoyed giving a course of Sunday night five-minute talks to the forces—"Things we laugh at" and "Just a moment, please!" were two of the titles. They were done at Bristol and it was great happiness to meet Ruth there, she coming from Cardiff for the occasion. The first time Diana heard me broadcast, at the age of three, she listened intently, said Ruth, and at the end asked, tearfully, "But how will he get out of the box?"

I

My first curacy was at St. John's, Newland, Hull, whose vicar was Canon A. E. Glover. What a superb parish priest he was! We got on famously. He taught me the duties of my office, setting me a most perfect example, and allowed me to preach constantly, when I believe I sometimes spoke as one inspired. Here I had experience of the German Blitz and shared in the anxiety, distress and suffering of the people. The port of Hull suffered considerably, as everyone knows.

Despite the work and the frequently disturbed nights, when the bombers came overhead in relays, I got through a lot of reading and did much writing. We had a small house, which Ruth made comfortable, and I spent all the time I could in my study. There I wrote several books and did quite a lot of journalism. I wrote weekly articles for the *Record*, under the heading of "The Watch Tower", but when it became known who the writer was, I changed it to

"D.R.D.'s Column" and continued it until the paper was amalgamated with *The Church of England Newspaper*, when, under the editorship of the Rev. C. O. Rhodes the column still went on, altogether, I think for something like nine years.

When Canon Glover retired I became acting vicar for some months, until the Rev. Frank Ford was offered and accepted the living. Frank and his intellectual wife, Eve, were our great friends during the war-time years. The Rev. John Stewart, vicar of St. Mary Lowgate, became Diana's godfather, and a wonderfully good friend to us all. Ah! if only I could tell of the many warm friends I made in Hull!

But I wanted to get to London, and when the living of Emmanuel, Dulwich, was offered to me I took it with joy, and had a very full life there, preaching, visiting, reading and writing. I was always being asked to preach, for now I had a Gospel which people wished to hear.

After four and a half happy years, I felt that I wanted to get into the country, and the Bishop of Chichester, ever a good friend, offered me the living of Holy Trinity, Ship Street, Brighton, the church that R. J. Campbell used to fill. It was a preaching church, with no parish duties, so that I was free to devote myself to writing. We had a charming house at Lindfield, sixteen miles from Brighton, where Ruth was very happy in a large garden with hens, fruit and vegetables. I was happy to watch her being so happy. She now had three children, for in addition to Diana, another daughter, Rachel Christiana, had been born in war-shocked Hull, and Richard Temple had come to us at Dulwich. Alec Vidler baptized the children and is Rachel's godfather. I published a book of sermons delivered at Holy Trinity, dedicated to the good friends I made there. What care I took over those sermons, yet somehow, they never drew the congregations I thought they deserved. I had to admit to myself that although the congregations gradually increased, my Brighton preaching was not a success. It was not backed by parish work, and somehow the life of the church had seemed entirely to have evaporated. I admit that this was a disappointment.

Preaching was and is a large part of my life, and at Brighton alone, of all the experiences I have ever had, I was, let me say frankly, a failure. Perhaps I expected too much, but whatever the cause, all virility seemed to go out of me in that pulpit. Fortunately this was restored elsewhere.

I was invited to preach at St. Paul's several times, and was amused to receive on each occasion a small cheque and half a bottle of sherry! Apparently the Lord Mayor used to entertain the morning preacher, and when this custom went out he substituted a bottle of sherry, and a fee sufficient to buy luncheon: later this was reduced to half a bottle of sherry, plus the fee! To me, the great St. Paul's was a cold church; I liked much better to be invited to Westminster Abbey, to which I went three times in one year, though this was against the rules.

2

While at Brighton, among other things, I published a monthly magazine inset called *Christian Renewal*, for the quality of the magazine material available for local church monthlies is notoriously poor. This was an immediate success and I continued it until another idea more in harmony with my particular outlook and love for preaching came to me, and in co-operation with my very good friend Selwyn Gummer, as co-editor, I started *Pulpit Monthly*. In this publication I found expression for the desire I had to raise the standard of preaching in the Anglican communion, especially to give help to parsons who felt (as I did not) the strain of preparing two sermons a week. This magazine proved its usefulness by a steadily increasing circulation throughout the English-speaking world wherever the Anglican Church had a footing. And not only Anglicans, but

ministers of all denominations are found among its sub-
scribers.

I used to preach without a note of any description, but I
prepared my sermons as all parsons must. Yet I gave very
little time, directly, to this preparation. Indirectly I gave
practically all my time, though, in a very real sense, my sermons are casual. I find they just happen. Of course I don't
waste my time. The themes are suggested by incidents in
contacts with my people, or by events, or by my Bible
reading. Once I have decided on theme and text (which
generally select themselves), I do nothing more about it.
I then carry on with my reading. On Saturday I turn the
subject over in my mind and endeavour to feel my way into
it. Once that is achieved all is well.

I am not presuming to suggest that this is a method to
copy. I am merely describing the method I happen to have
evolved myself. I rarely write sermons, except for broadcasting, when I have no choice, and very special occasions
on which the theme is dictated to me. Latterly, however,
I have used notes regularly, and at times have even written
out my sermons word for word. Also, always, whenever I
could I went over the sermon aloud, either alone in the
country, with no one about, or in my study. I have had
Ruth as my single audience, more than once!

I once asked a famous and prolific writer (G. D. H.
Cole) how many words a day he usually wrote. His answer
staggered me—anything from 8,000 to 10,000. He assured
me that he wrote every word. He did not dictate. How did
he manage it? I once did 5,000 words in one day, but it took
me nineteen hours to do it, and I was utterly useless for a
week afterwards. I think an average of 4,000 words a day
is good going for a short period—say a fortnight. But that
means a fourteen-hour day. It is the thinking that takes the
time. I think out what I am going to write thoroughly
before putting pen to paper. Some writers tell me that they
think by means of writing, with the result that they are

constantly re-writing. Perhaps I ought to revise more than I do, but the fact is that my revision is done before the writing. That is Irish, but it is true. I work out the idea, argument, or description as clearly as I can: it then writes itself.

I have two lines of study on which I have been working quietly for several years, and which I hope to turn into books some time before I die. I like to think, moreover, that they will be genuine contributions to Christian thinking—probably a vain hope. The first is a study of the influence of economic and political factors on the development of Christian doctrine and ethics. The second, a study of the political and social implications of Original Sin, or as I prefer to call it, Radical Sin.

Hundreds of Histories of Christian Doctrine have been written from time to time. I do not know a single book which attempts to show how the general development of Christian doctrine as a whole was affected by political and economic conflicts and interests. Of the many Christian scholars I have consulted, not one could put me on to such a study. Not even the Archbishop, to whom I mentioned the matter, knew of such a book, and there are few men whose scholarship is more comprehensive. Neither was Dr. Micklem aware of such a work. There have been attempts at studying the political and economic influences on particular doctrines as, for instance, Dr. Shailer Matthews' *The Atonement and Social Process*. But with due respect to so great a scholar, I think it a poor book, for it fails in appreciation of the dynamic interpenetration of politics, economics and culture, which is one of the Marxist contributions to Christian thinking. There are, too, scattered hints in a number of writers—Niebuhr, Rauchenbusch, Engels, Calhoun. But not a single specific comprehensive study.

I am convinced that without a knowledge of political and economic factors the study of the history of doctrine is abstract and deceptive. We know a little bit more today of the process of "rationalization", by means of which we clothe our basic egoism in a garb of altruism and virtue. The same process is operative in the formation of Christian doctrine. To trace the political and economic factors is to uncover the basic egotism from which no human activity is completely free—not even the most exalted doctrinal speculations. Some vested interest or other has played a part in the original formulation of every cultural expression. Christian doctrine is no exception. Thus such a study would have not only a scientific value, but a very important moral and spiritual value. It would help the student to cultivate a sense of humility and self-knowledge. And what a vast difference that would make in the relative situations of history! The man who is aware of the play of egotism in his own attitude or theory will be less harsh in his judgment of opponents and less brutal and cruel in his treatment of them.

Closely allied is this vast question of the implications for politics and social progress of the doctrine of Radical Sin. Given the fact of Radical Sin, what does it involve in terms of political development, of economic institutions, of historic growth? In short, what is the sociology of Radical Sin? It may sound fantastic to the theological reader to say that this aspect of Radical Sin has hardly been touched. But it is true. It raises acutely the whole question of the ground of Christian participation in politics. The answer of the so-called "Social Gospel" to this problem is incredibly shallow. The recognition of the fact of Radical Sin necessitates a drastic revision of the Christian attitude to politics.

Here are some of the fundamental questions in which I am deeply interested.

Now, it is obvious that the pursuit of these two immense problems demands time and energy for systematic, painstaking, disciplined research and reading. It cannot be effectively done in odd moments or hours. Martin Luther, in advocating the jealous use of the stray problem, confessed that he made good use of his time when he "was on my business in the privy". He did two things at the same time. I dare say one can get through a lot of reading in a lavatory, though I have never tried it. I have sedulously avoided mixing two such opposites. It is quite certain, however, that systematic research into such vast problems cannot be done in this way, or by any other method of snatching at "the unforgiving moment". It requires the leisure of deep thought.

3

Somehow or other, I never found the leisure at Brighton, so that after two and a half years when I was offered the living of St. Mary Magdalen, St. Leonards-on-Sea, a large church, with a large though poorly-conditioned vicarage, close to the sea, I took it. Once again I was plunged into parish work, and the personal contacts it involved uplifted my heart. Also I found that my preaching, being given a new inspiration perhaps, appealed to the congregation, which was always good, and, during the summer months when the town was crowded with holiday makers, more than filled the church, Sunday after Sunday.

One day, after a sermon on "Humour" I was approached after the service by a German visitor with tears streaming down his face. He said, "You have touched my heart; I want to hear more," and there and then invited me to Germany for six weeks. Ruth and I both went, and stayed for three weeks at his delightful home near Münster. It was a great adventure, for we were kindred spirits, talking well into the night on many very similar interests. While with my friend I took advantage of his kindness to pay a visit to Wittenberg to see the church where Martin Luther preached and the door of the castle church on which he nailed his ninety-five propositions. Though in the Russian zone, it was worth it.

After nearly nine happy and fulfilled years at Hastings the

urge to get free from the absorbing duties of a large parish, and to devote myself in the years that remained to me to the writing I most desire to do, became too strong to be resisted. So I asked the Bishop if there were any possibility of a small country parish, and I have now heard of a tiny church in the middle of a park at the foot of the South Downs in West Sussex, needing an incumbent. Ruth and I have been to see it and have fallen wholly in love with it. There are three very little churches, Parham, Wiggonholt and Greatham, united in a single living, which the Hon. Clive Pearson has offered me. How grateful I am to him, and how much I look forward to this new life and to the work I hope to be able to accomplish there.

So I draw to the end of my story. It may or may not be continued. It is unwise to look too far into the future in our present situation. Today, more than of the normal condition of our existence here, it is true to say that "in the midst of life we are in death". So for the present my narrative closes.

I have tried to show the reader how one human being in this twentieth century has grown from childhood to old age. It has been a story of great vicissitudes, of alternating success and failure, of frustration and despair, which sank to the abyss: but a story of renewal, of re-birth into hope and faith, the story of a new man.

In what does the significance of such a narrative consist? Were this the story of merely one isolated human individual, it would not have been worth the telling. Rightly or wrongly, I am persuaded that my story is the microcosm of a generation. Here on the smaller scale of an individual existence can be studied the history of an era—except, at present, for the conclusion. I experienced in my soul the bitter death of the illusions of the generation into which I was born, and lost myself in those illusions. But after that death I rose again, for I found myself in finding God. What I was searching for was my own identity, and without knowing it my search was for God. I had to give up myself exactly as I was, in the chaos and disillusion into which I had fallen, to find Him. I found Him and became a new man.

I have mentioned the name of Martin Luther, and it is not strange that in these later years I have been drawn to an intimate study of his works, for I have found in him a likeness to myself. I too believe in total sin and total salvation. Like him I have suffered a lifelong burden of guilt. I was acquainted with the backside of life. His father was a miner as mine was, and I started work in the mine as he did. I had love of music, amorous thoughts, at times a vast appetite, craving for beer, the sense of a personal Devil, a liking for bawdy jokes, and I suffered from constipation. I spend more and more hours reading him. He is my elder brother.

The generation to which I belong has exhausted the illusion of modern civilization, the civilization which took its rise in the Renaissance. This is the profound, ultimate fact of our time. The magnificent alternative with which della Mirandola challenged European man 400 years ago, to become beast or angel, has still to be decided.

My generation emptied life of faith and belief, not merely in Christianity, but still more in the substitutes for Christianity. So the new generation is left only the bitter lees, nihilism, nescience and unfaith. Will there be faith found on the earth? It is to this great question that my story gives the answer, and the only finally satisfying answer. This, I believe, is the significance of my narrative. In the eternal, historic New Testament Gospel there is power to meet the need of man.

Our age has not yet come to the last despair. In that I have anticipated it. On that late August night on the Southern-down beach, I drank the cup of anguish to its last bitter dregs. To that cup our world must come. In final, utter despair lies its great hope, despair of its own pride and power. Our age must be told again and again in trumpet tones, that God lives. If the men of today can come to believe that, even remotely, coldly, if they can enter the dark valley of Achor with only a pin-point of belief that there is God, they will find Him as Redeemer, when their pride is broken. Despair of self is not to be feared. It is to be prayed for. I had to suffer, to make myself suffer, to be abandoned. I had to go into hell. Every kind of nastiness had to be mine. I had to experience God's angry cloud. My justification is not in me, for I am a sinner, a sinner, a sinner. My justification is in Christ, I am justified by faith, for I have no merit, not a scrap; in myself I die, in Christ I am made alive. I can ask no greater blessing for my wearied, disillusioned generation than the blessing of despair; for in it they will meet Him who will save them "to the uttermost".

INDEX

oks a   h   rned   four